rainbow year

Moira Andrew

Winter Twigs, see page 40

Line drawings by Andrea Heath

First Published in 1994 by
BELAIR PUBLICATIONS LIMITED
P.O. Box 12, Twickenham, TW1 2QL
England
© 1994 Moira Andrew
Series Editor Robyn Gordon
Designed by Richard Souper
Photography by Kelvin Freeman and Linton Lowe
Typesetting by Belair
Printed and Bound in Hong Kong by World Print Ltd
ISBN 0 947882 38 3

Acknowledgements

The author and publishers would like to give special thanks to the staff of Dinas Powys Infant School, Cardiff, and Malpas Church Junior School, Newport, for their generous help and support during the preparation of *Rainbow Year.* They also wish to thank the children of these schools for their hard work and unfailing enthusiasm.

They would like to thank Malpas Park Primary School, Newport; Llanfihangel Rhydithon County Primary School, Llandrindod Wells, and Franksbridge County Primary School, Llandrindod Wells, for their contributions to the children's work shown in this book.

They would also like to thank Lucy Allen and Kate Hindley for the cover artwork.

Winter Window, see page 40

Contents

Salt Dough models, instructions on page 72

Introduction

Rainbow Year aims to provide a resource bank of ideas for topics linked to poetry around the school year. The book is divided into eleven sections, September through to July, highlighting assemblies and creative activities appropriate to each season.

Many of the poems have been specially written for *Rainbow Year* and the poets have tried to reflect weathers, festivals and feelings associated with the passing months. The assembly themes are suitable for children at all levels of the primary school and many of the creative activities can be adapted up or down, across the age range. We have tried to include examples of children's work at every stage.

I am particularly interested in children's writing and often use poetry as a starting point. It is recognised that the process of writing is as important as the finished work, so I suggest that the children's independent writing should follow the general pattern of planning (listing) to drafting, to revising. This is where the *teaching* element takes place. The final presentation should be as near-perfect as each individual child can make it.

I find that children tend to work at their best when they are offered a structure or way-in to the writing task. In my experience, the time spent on oral work where teacher and children pool their ideas, pays handsome dividends. A word of warning: don't be tempted to put every idea on the blackboard - too much choice baffles some young writers. I use the 'borrow one, find one' idea when children are asked to write out their initial list of words and phrases.

It is important to encourage children to try out different ways of presenting their completed work (wall display? tape? book? anthology? drama?) and to keep the notion of audience in mind. The young authors should feel that writing is an exciting and worthwhile activity, one which they can approach with a measure of success. Be lavish with congratulations on a successfully completed piece of work. I find that success breeds success.

I hope that teachers will enjoy dipping into the ideas suggested in *Rainbow Year* and that they will feel able to adapt and expand the possibilities to fit their own individual ways of working.

Moira Andrew

The Christmas Story, see page 29

September

Strange Fruit
If purple pears hung on the tree
and gooseberries were pink
if strawberries were white as milk
and apples blue as ink,

if plums grew silver as the moon
and cherries like the sun,
I wouldn't leave them in the bowl
I'd eat up every one.
Irene Rawnsley

The First Day with a New Teacher
Today
We are new.
Nameless
Part of the corporate
'You lot.'

Tomorrow
We will clamour
For our identities
And
Your attention.
John Coldwell

Where was the colour Orange born?
This colour orange
where was it born?
Was it born in the sky
on a summer's dawn?

Or maybe one day
you saw God spill
his red and yellow
over some hill?

No, it was dusk.

And as the sun
sank over the corn,
in the autumn sky
here orange was born!
Judith Nicholls

Blackberries
Today we found blackberries in the wood.
Blackberries are very good,
a lovely, juicy, tangy taste -
we don't let blackberries go to waste!
Charles Thomson

TALKING TOGETHER
New term, new faces: September is the start of the new school year, new teacher perhaps, new friends, new surroundings. Read John Coldwell's 'The First Day with a New Teacher'.

● If the teacher is new to the class, she might talk about her own family, hobbies, pets etc. Bring a few photographs, a favourite book, a treasured object from home. Listen with the children to music on tape. Introduce oneself as a *person*, not just a teacher.
● Encourage individual children to introduce themselves in a similar way, talking for about five minutes. Ask them to bring a book, a photograph, a favourite toy, something connected with their hobby. They should have time to prepare what they are going to say. This task helps give confidence in speaking aloud.
● Talk about names, how important names are as part of one's identity. Look at a book of names for new babies. Discuss the origins of each child's first name. Talk about family names: how *Thatcher, Butcher, Forester* derived from specific occupations; how *Mc* and *O'* mean 'son of'; how some surnames are common to particular regions, e.g. *Jones, Thomas, Evans* in Wales.
● Talk about goals - how important it is to plan. Let the children write down three things they would like to achieve during the school year - *possible, probable* and *quite outrageous!*
Seal the slips of paper away in an envelope and don't open until July.

ASSEMBLIES
● **Michaelmas:** Following discussions about new beginnings for the school year, the children can join in Michaelmas celebrations (29th September). It used to be a time when farmers gave thanks for the harvest and looked forward to a new year on the farm. Mop fairs were held at which farm hands were hired for the year ahead. It was a time of feasting and dance.

- Hold your own Mop Fair with folk dancing, music and dressing up, stressing that it is important to make time for fun and enjoyment after work well done. Find out all you can about harvest rituals.
- **Passports:** Teachers can bring and talk about their passports. Get the children to design their own passports to the new school year. What should it contain? Photograph or portrait, special characteristics, hobbies, goals. Ask children to add their own short prayer for the new session.

GROUP ACTIVITIES

- **September colour:** Look at trees, hedgerows, gardens. Talk about the colours of late summer. What is the predominant colour?

- Read 'Where was the colour Orange born?' by Judith Nicholls. Talk about all the orange, golden, yellow things that appear this month. Make a gold display using leaves, flowers, fruit. Add a few articles made of 'gold': coins, medals, junk jewellery, perhaps spilling from a treasure chest.

- Read Irene Rawnsley's 'Strange Fruit'. Think of unusual, *unreal* colours for fruit and vegetables. Do you think that this might change the taste, or make it magic? Would you enjoy vegetables more? (See Art Activities.)

- Look for pictures of sunflowers or, even better, bring one in from the garden. Look at the structure of the petals, the way the seeds grow in a spiral. Look at the colours, from bright yellow to glowing bronze. Look at a print of Van Gogh's famous sunflowers.
  Van Gogh loved sunflowers, their warmth, their vibrant colours. In 1889 he wrote, 'I am thinking of decorating my studio with half a dozen pictures of sunflowers...a decoration in which chrome yellow, crude or broken, shall blaze forth against different backgrounds...like Gothic stained glass windows.'
  Discuss why you think Van Gogh thought his sunflowers would 'blaze forth'. What other hot words can you find to describe the colour of sunflowers (glow, burn, flare, shine)? Make a word wheel of fiery words and phrases.

- Look for ripe blackberries on the hedgerows. The children may be able to pick enough blackberries to make jam. Look at how fingers are stained with juice. Taste the sharpness of the fruit. Read 'Blackberries' by Charles Thomson. He says that they have 'a lovely juicy tangy taste'. Make a list of other taste words to describe ripe blackberries.

- Charles Thomson says that we should not let the blackberries go to waste. What could we do with them (bake pies, make jam)? Follow the Blackberry and Apple Jam recipe and bake brown bread to go with it. Have a slice of fresh bread with blackberry and apple jam. Describe the taste and the smell.

Blackberry and Apple Jam

2lb blackberries
5 fluid oz water
1lb cooking apples
3lb preserving sugar

Method: Wash blackberries. Peel, core and slice apples. Put fruit and water in a pan. Cook until tender. Add sugar and stir over a low heat until dissolved. Bring to the boil and cook rapidly. When setting point is reached (after about 15 minutes) take pan off heat. Skim and pour carefully into hot dry jars. Cover and label when cool.

Van Gogh thought his sunflowers should 'blaze forth'. The children copied one of his pictures

● **This colour gold:** Read Judith Nicholls' 'Where was the colour Orange born?' Look at the gold of autumn leaves, of corn, of sunflowers and rudbeckia, or autumn sunshine. Follow the pattern of the poem and make up a new one suggesting magical ideas about where the colour gold might have been born. Extend this to other autumn colours: the purple of blackberries, the red of rosehips, the brown of fallen leaves.

WRITING ACTIVITIES
● **Nature diary:** Begin a nature diary. Make it one which will last for the school year, so take time to design substantial covers. Discuss an overall title, for example, *Wild Things*, *Seasons, Through the Year*. Look for changes to trees and plants in the school grounds, in the hedgerows, in the local park. Make notes and sketches. Date your entries. (See book-making instructions on the following page.)

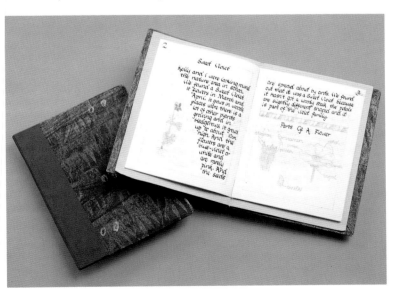

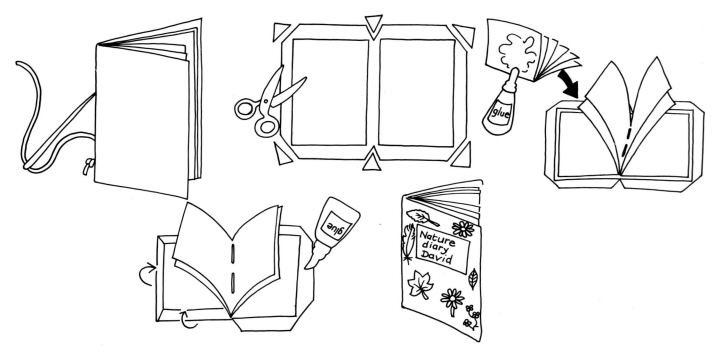

Making a book: see Nature Diary on previous page

● **Factfile:** Read John Coldwell's 'The First Day with a New Teacher'. He says that the class is part of a nameless 'you lot'. Design a Factfile to make you stand out as an individual. Fill in the facts first: name (with a self-portrait), address, date of birth, members of the family.

Now add some personal likes and dislikes, things which make you stand out from the crowd: your hobbies, pets (real and imagined - perhaps you would like to take a green dragon for a walk!), things you like/don't like to eat, your favourite music/television programmes, words and phrases that you use (over-use?), things you would *never* say.

Story writers and novelists often base their characters on real people, but they change the names and 'embroider' the facts a little.

Swap your Factfile with someone else in your group. Each of you can write a pen portrait of the other, using some of the details in the file, but changed to make them more interesting or funnier to read, like a character in an adventure story.

● **Apples/Plums/Pears:** If you have an apple/plum/pear tree in the garden, bring in some fallen fruit and taste it. Find recipes for plum chutney or plum jam, apple tart or apple sauce etc. After you have tried them out, make up a class recipe book. Parents and grandparents might be glad to help in finding old family recipes. Using coloured pencils or felt-tip pens, decorate each page with a border of fruit.

Read Charles Thomson's poem 'Blackberries'. Using it as a pattern, write about apples, plums and pears in the same way. Find the best words to describe the taste and texture of the fruit.

● **Autumn diary:** Imagine that you are a squirrel, hedgehog, field mouse. Write your diary for a week in September, noting all the precious nuts and seeds that you have found for your winter store. Suggest secret places where you can hide your hoard. Make it a tiny book.

A zig-zag book - see The Colour Orange on page 10

● **Strange Fruit:** Read Irene Rawnsley's poem 'Strange Fruit'. Imagine waking up one morning and looking out of your bedroom window to see blue apples and silver pears growing on the trees. Turn this into the beginning of an adventure story. Are you in a magic orchard? Have you landed on a faraway planet? Perhaps you are in a wizard's garden! Invent characters to people your story. Give them names, describe what they look like, what they wear, how they speak. Write about your adventures in the land of magic fruit. (Do you remember the story of *Jack and the Beanstalk?*) Tell how you get back home - with a silver plum or a golden cherry to give to your mum!

ART ACTIVITIES

● **Us Lot!:** Read John Coldwell's poem about the first day with a new teacher. Paint a self-portrait, just head and shoulders (about A4 size), or work in pairs to paint a picture of your friend. Cut out the portraits and glue on a background, collage-style. Add a speech bubble to give your name. Now you are no longer the nameless 'You lot!' of the poem. Call your frieze 'Us Lot!'

● **Jack-in-the-Box Names:** Take a piece of card - long if your name is Katherine, short if it is Tony. Outline your name in capital letters using 'bubble writing'. Push the letters close together so that the white paper is almost hidden. Use felt-tip pens to pattern each letter, then cut out round the shape made by your name. Fix each on to a thin plant stick and push the sticks into Plasticine inside an open box, as shown.

9

● **Apple Trees mobile:** Use two teaplates of different sizes to make your template. Draw the tree to fit inside the circle, but touching it in several places. Use sharp-pointed scissors, or a craft knife on a self-sealing board, to cut out the shape. Turn the mobile over and add details, gluing on leaves, apples etc. Punch the top edge with a file-punch, and thread through a loop of matching cotton.

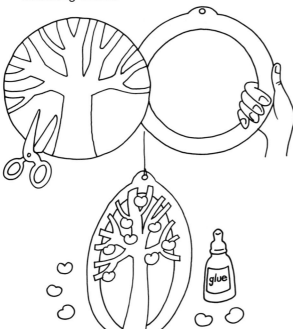

● **Magic Tree:** Read or listen to Irene Rawnsley's 'Strange Fruit'. Use thin card to make and cut out the outline of a tall tree with lots of bare branches. The tree should reach as near to the ceiling as is possible. Now make 'magic' fruit to hang on the branches. Have plums, pears, apples etc. all together on the one tree. Cover some of the fruit with silver and gold paper. Paint other fruit shapes with patterns, stripes, zig-zags and spots. Make everything as zany and exciting as you can.

● **September Gold:** Paint a frieze of autumn trees. Some leaves should be green, some gold, a few orange and red. Now paint and cut out lots of golden leaves. Thread them on cotton and tape them to the top of the picture. Tape the other end to the display table showing books open at suitable autumn pages, so that the gold leaves look as though they are 'whirling, twirling, swirling' from the trees.
● Make up a movement dance of falling leaves. Dress in yellow shifts or hold big gold cut-out leaves in your hands.

● **The Colour Orange:** Using cartridge paper, make a zig-zag book and write out Judith Nicholls' poem, one verse to each page. Use coloured pencils or felt-tip pens to illustrate each verse. Make up an extra verse to match the others. When you have written your own colour poems in the same style as Judith Nicholls (see Language Activities), make zig-zag books and illustrate in the same way (see photograph of children's work on page 9).

● **Sunflowers:** Look at a print of Van Gogh's 'Sunflowers'. Look at the way he paints each separate petal. Paint a large sunflower head using thick bright yellow poster colour. Make each petal by painting one firm stroke away from the centre. Paint rows of overlapping petals. When the flowers are dry, cut out and mass together, either as a field of sunflowers stretching into the distance, or as a few flowers in a vase, the way Van Gogh has done. Experiment with different coloured backgrounds - sometimes Van Gogh used blue, sometimes yellow, sometimes a grey-green.
Copy the picture as faithfully as possible (see photograph on page 7). Frame each one and hang as a group in the hall to make an art gallery of sunflower paintings.

October

Jack o'Lantern
Aglow with amber light
a grinning pumpkin face
with slits for smiles
and a lighted candle
flickering fluttering
dancing in its shadow.
Michael Henry

leaf-birds
leaves in a tumble
whirl about the branch
leaves in the autumn
twirl and dance

round and down they flutter
scatter everywhere
orange-brown birds
swirling through the air.
Joan Poulson

October
O for the owls that call from the night,
C for the crows fast-flying out of sight,
T for the trees that are shedding their leaves,
O for the oak as for summer it grieves,
B for the berries so sweet and so black,
E for the elms that wither and crack,
R for the robins who always come back.

AUTUMN the season that lets in the cold,
OCTOBER the month when the year grows old.
Moira Andrew

Autumn Treasure
Seeds on the wind
travelling in the air,
seeds on parachutes
twirling everywhere.

Seeds from pepperpots
shaken on the ground,
seeds like catapults
shooting all around.

Seeds bright as jewels,
seeds on the wing,
seeds buried in the earth
ready for the spring.
Moira Andrew

Diwali
Fetch the candles.
Make it bright.
This is *our* festival
of light.

The goddess is coming
with luck and treats.
There's going to be laughter,
fireworks and sweets.

Family and friends
are together tonight.
For this is Diwali,
our festival of light.
Tony Mitton

(Diwali is celebrated in either October or November)

TALKING TOGETHER

- **Harvest Thanksgiving:** October is traditionally the time for thanking God for 'all good gifts around us'. Much useful discussion can arise from this theme: Where does our food come from? Set up classroom displays (using labels, empty packets, pictures, advertisements) or home-produced food, food which comes from other countries, food which is bought ready to cook/eat. (See also Art/Writing Activities.)
- Talk about different kinds of food to build strong bodies: milk, fruit, vegetables, fish, eggs, meat. Discuss the pros and cons of vegetarianism.
- Stress how lucky we are to have enough food. Talk about those children who have only one meal a day - if that. Older juniors can explore reasons for famine, make a news album, organise a fund-raising event to send money to charities working with children.

- **Autumn Seeds:** Read 'Autumn Treasure' by Moira Andrew. Make a collection of autumn seeds. Put them into categories determined by the way in which they are distributed. Look for 'pepperpot' seeds, e.g. poppy, 'parachute' seeds, e.g. sycamore, seeds 'bright as jewels', e.g. rosehips. Look for conkers and acorns. Can you find a description for seeds like this? (See Writing Activities.)

ASSEMBLIES

- **Harvest Thanksgiving:** Many schools will hold some form of Thanksgiving celebration for harvest during the month of October.
- Make a table display of flowers and fruit, vegetables and canned goods, cakes and bread, jam and pickles. Display corn sheaves, corn dollies, farm implements. Write poems and prayers of thanks for harvest.
- Encourage children to think of different harvests - of corn, of the hedgerows, of the sea. Think of the long hours of labour involved in farming, of the dangers which fishermen face.
- Invite pensioners to a simple breakfast of cereals, home-made bread and jam with coffee or tea. The children can play host and invite their visitors to stay on and take part in the Harvest Thanksgiving celebration. Make up small, brightly-decorated parcels of fruit, biscuits and tea bags as harvest gifts for the pensioners.

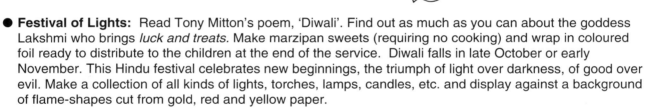

- **Harvest of the Sea:** Schools located near the sea might wish to centre their Harvest Festival on fish and fishing. Decorate the hall with nets and floats and a collage of silver-foil fish. The fish is one of the earliest Christian symbols, so the children might design a hanging prayer, edged with fish shapes to give thanks to the men of the sea for their courage and to pray for their safety.
- **Blessing the Waters:** Visit the local harbour, if possible. Make flower garlands and follow the ancient custom of throwing them into the waves as a prayer of thanks for the harvest of the sea. Less dramatically, the garlands are sometimes placed in church to ask God to bless the fishermen and keep them safe. This ceremony could be part of the harvest service for schools in a fishing community. (See display photograph on facing page.

- **Festival of Lights:** Read Tony Mitton's poem, 'Diwali'. Find out as much as you can about the goddess Lakshmi who brings *luck and treats.* Make marzipan sweets (requiring no cooking) and wrap in coloured foil ready to distribute to the children at the end of the service. Diwali falls in late October or early November. This Hindu festival celebrates new beginnings, the triumph of light over darkness, of good over evil. Make a collection of all kinds of lights, torches, lamps, candles, etc. and display against a background of flame-shapes cut from gold, red and yellow paper.
At the beginning of a service of thanks for the power of light, close the blinds and light a single candle. Talk about how one candle can light up the darkness. Have a table laid with night lights and get children to light them one by one until the hall is lit by candle flame. (Careful adult supervision is necessary.) Sitar music can be played on tape as the children move quietly to the front and back to their places. It is very effective - further enhanced if saris can be shown and worn (perhaps by a Hindu mother). (See Art Activities.)

- **Moon Cake Festival:** This is a Chinese harvest festival to celebrate the moon goddess. Prayers are written on scraps of paper and concealed inside sweet cakes call Moon Cakes. Make shining moon mobiles from silver foil. Let the children write mini-harvest prayers on stamp-sized paper and hide them underneath small portions of sponge cake - iced and decorated with a moon-goddess' face. Sing harvest songs and read out some of the prayers.

Blessing the Waters, see facing page

GROUP ACTIVITIES

● **Autumn seeds:** Follow up the oral work on autumn seeds by displaying each category or set on the nature table in a P.E. hoop or glued within a coloured ring on backing paper. Encourage children to identify tree seeds from information books. This task is like a treasure hunt, leading children to work systematically from clue to clue towards eventual identification. It also gives practice in the skills of information retrieval.

● Dry seeds and paste them into your nature diary. Draw the tree to which they belong. Label and date your drawings.

● Find dandelion clocks and blow the seeds away (see Art Activities). Watch how they float and fly. Make up a movement dance to show the way seeds twirl and scatter. Use percussion instruments to make music for your autumn seed dance.

● **Autumn leaves:** Look for a suitable deciduous tree in the school grounds. Let the children work in pairs, choosing and tagging one particular leaf which is still attached to the branch. Note how it changes in colour. Find a fallen leaf from the same tree.

● **Make a zig-zag book from cartridge paper.** Using the fallen leaf as a stencil, draw an outline on each page. Studying their own named leaf, the children use coloured pencils to fill in the first outline, making the colours as accurate as possible. Date the picture. Follow the changes over the next few weeks to make a colour record of an individual leaf.

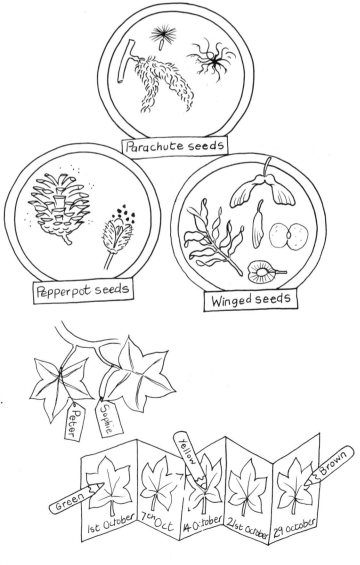

- Discuss in a group if, for example, beech leaves change at a different rate from sycamores, how the colours differ, and the date on which the last leaf fell.

- **Hallowe'en:** The celebration of Hallowe'en (or All Hallows' Eve) dates back to ancient times. On the last day of October people used to dress up, light bonfires and make pumpkin or turnip lanterns to scare away bad spirits before All Hallows' Day dawned.

- Discuss with the children what makes them frightened (going to bed upstairs alone, 'things that go BUMP in the night', getting lost). Talk about ways of coping with fear, and share ideas. (If appropriate, this could be a time to set up an anonymous 'bully box' where children can bring their fears about bullying to the attention of the adults in the school.)

- Read Michael Henry's 'Jack o' Lantern', and make some lanterns in school. Try to give them grinning faces and *slits for smiles*. Failing real turnip lanterns (and they are a bit messy!), make Jack o'Lanterns from papier mâché-covered balloons. Paint them vivid orange and decorate with black smiling mouths. Don't, of course, put a candle inside - it's too dangerous. (See Writing Activities.)

WRITING ACTIVITIES

- **Taste of autumn:** October is the month when we get the first 'taste of autumn'. The sun isn't quite so warm, the leaves begin their autumn dance, the days are shorter.

- Make a list of changes, e.g. apples ripening, leaves changing colour, birds preparing to fly south, etc. Put them together, taking a new line for each idea, and a poem will grow. Begin each verse with a different 'taste'. Your poem might look like this:

  Taste autumn on the wind
  when apples ripen on the tree
  and.......................................

  Taste autumn in the woods
  when leaves are painted gold
  and.......................................

- Everyone can borrow the same first line to get the poem started. Think of other 'tastings', *on the hills, in the sky,* etc.

- **Jack o' Lantern:** Read Michael Henry's 'Jack o' Lantern'. Make a lantern with a fierce/sad/angry face. (See Group Activities.) Imagine that you could ask questions of this pumpkin face. Find ten questions, going for magic and mystery, for example,

  Who are you?
  Where do you go in summer time?
  Are you dead or alive?

Work with a partner and write down questions and answers to form a dialogue. Make it the basis of a spooky story (or play) where Jack o' Lantern is the main character. Set the story in a dark forest or a ruined castle.

- **October acrostic:** Read Moira Andrew's 'October' and use it as a pattern for an acrostic poem of your own. Write the word OCTOBER downwards and begin each line of your poem with the letters in order. Each line should describe something special about the month: the games you play, the weather, the colours you see around you, what animals do in autumn. Remember - your poem doesn't have to rhyme!

- **Things that go Bump in the Night.** Make a list of all the frightening things that you might think of in the dark: snakes, ghosts, monsters. Now use them to make a funny poem - nothing like making fun of your fears to chase them away! Add the chorus, *I'm not afraid of the dark, not me!'* and write the final version of your poem in the middle of the paper. Use another sheet to make a frame and glue over your poem.

- **Harvest prayers:** Beginning with a simple *Thank you for* enough food to eat; move on to prayers for fishermen or farmers or people who cook for us, etc.
  If the prayers rhyme, they can be set to music. (See Assemblies.)

- Mount the prayers and hang them like Chinese banners in hall or corridor. (They look even better displayed outdoors from the branch of a tree, but the success of the idea depends on the weather!)

- **Invitations:** If the children invite visitors to their Harvest celebration, they might make and illustrate invitation cards to the event. The cards should be personal to the recipient and individually addressed. (See Assemblies.)

- **Autumn seeds:** Read 'Autumn Treasure'. Look closely at the seeds you have gathered. (See Group Activities.) Find movement words to describe the way different seeds are dispersed. For the youngest children this can be built up into a simple list poem, for example,

  parachute seeds twirling
  catapult seeds shooting

  Add a chorus at the end of each two lines, for example,
  autumn winds blowing seeds
  all across the land.

'parachute seeds twirling'

● **Autumn leaves:** Read Joan Poulson's 'leaf-birds'. She says that leaves turn into *orange-brown birds* as they flutter in the wind. Watch the way falling leaves move in the wind. Make a collection of movement words, e.g. *twirling, swirling, dancing.* Using 'leaf-birds' as a pattern, write a 'copycat' poem imagining that the leaves have turned into something different - *bronze butterflies,* for example. It might look like this:

> *leaf-butterflies*
>
> *leaves in a whirl*
> *dancing in the air,*
> *bronze-bright butterflies*
> *floating everywhere*

You must, of course, choose something that floats or flies if your copycat poem is to work.

ART ACTIVITIES
● **Mobiles:** Read 'leaf-birds'. Make mobiles to go with this poem, using instructions as for the mobile on page 10. Decorate with falling leaves in red, yellow and orange. (See photograph above.)
● Make dandelion clock mobiles in a similar way. (See photograph on previous page.)

● **Festival of lights:** Against a dark background paste huge flame shapes, collage-style, red, orange, yellow and gold. Put a single large white candle-shape in the centre. Drape with a bright sari and place a collection of lights/lamps on the display table below. (See Assemblies)

● **Harvest basket:** Look at the collection of vegetables on the Harvest table. Study shape and colour. On sugar paper, paint one vegetable each. Make it big and bright. Cut out the vegetable when the paint is dry and pile, collage-style, into a cut-out basket shape. Use as a harvest asssembly frieze. Use the same idea for a harvest basket mobile.

● **Blessing the Waters:** Make a sea background on frieze paper. This can be in wave bands of colour: blue, green, turquoise and silver, made as a mosaic. From tissue paper, make brightly-coloured garlands to 'float' on the waves. Add little fishing boats tossing about in the distance. (See display photograph on page 13.)

November

November

November is a grey road
Cloaked in mist.
A twist of wood-smoke
In the gathering gloom.
A scurrying squirrel
Hoarding acorns
A steel-grey river
Glinting in the twilight.
A grey rope
Knotted around a threadbare tree.
John Foster

Bonfire Night Lights

```
         H!
        S
       O
      O
     O
    O
   O
  W
```
November the Fifth
and a fountain of fireworks,
brightly splatters its colours
across a black paper sky.

Underneath,
hurrying silhouettes
race along half lit streets,
searching the Bonfire Night celebrations.

While high above
the sky's own firework stars,
pinprick the blackness
and like tiny torches offer to light the way.
Ian Souter

Autumn Sorrow

The moon sobs
  open-mouthed
and stars hang
  like tears
on the cheeks of night.
Moira Andrew

Fireworks

Fiery flowers
  blossoming
   in the night sky
like prize chrysanthemums,
silver and blue, red and gold.
They melt into darkness,
  sparks falling
  as brief petals
  on the wind.
Moira Andrew

Sky Arrows

```
                    arrow
                 birds
            migrating
         by
      play
              their                    flying
           games                       off
             and                       to
          wave                      warmer
        goodbye                    lands
                             over
                          crimson
                           forests
                            and
                              amber
                                sands
```
John Walsh

TALKING TOGETHER

● **Shorter days/Longer nights:** Talk about what one can do in the long evenings - a time for reading, hobbies, watching television and videos. Exchange ideas for 'an evening well-spent'. Talk about how children feel inside their own homes, curtains drawn, warm and well-fed. Discuss those less fortunate than themselves. The children might consider fund-raising, e.g. for *Save the Children* (perhaps from a Christmas concert or school jumble sale).

● **Sharing our lives:** Talk about beginning a correspondence with schools in a different environment - where the winters are colder, or where November means summertime. Decide what questions to ask, what the children would tell of their own lives: school, games, weather, clothes, etc. (See Writing Activities.)

- **Bonfire Night:** Read Ian Souter's poem 'Bonfire Night Lights'. Tell the story of Guy Fawkes, of how he tried to blow up the Parliament buildings in 1605. Find rhymes and poems about Guy Fawkes.
- A day or so before the date, discuss how the children are going to celebrate Bonfire Night. Talk about the need for safety in handling fireworks, about how frightened dogs and cats can be, about how busy fire crews, the police and hospital accident units are on November 5th. Suggest that children draw up their own rules for safety. (See Group Activities.)

ASSEMBLIES
- **Remembrance Day:** Although many schools sell poppies, the reasons behind Remembrance Day are difficult concepts for young children to deal with. Of course, they know something of war from news reports on television, so perhaps it is best to take a positive view, stressing our thankfulness for peace and freedom.
- Tell the children about the poppies growing blood-red on the graves of soldiers in France. Look at black and white photographs of wartime. Talk about what was happening. Listen to parts of Britten's 'War Requiem' and a few lines from the First World War poets, for example,

  In Flanders fields the poppies blow
  Between the crosses, row on row........(John McCrae)
- Have a minute's silence to think about how lucky we are to live in a time of peace. Make a frieze of poppies to illustrate John McCrae's lines. (See Art Activities.)

- **St Andrew's Day:** Tell the story of St Andrew, who is thought to have been one of the disciples of Jesus. St Andrew is the patron saint of Scotland and, when he died, his bones were taken to Scotland and St Andrew's Cathedral was built over his grave.
- On 30th November, the children can be invited to wear something tartan: scarf, hat, skirt. Sing a Scottish folksong, listen to a tape of bagpipe music, or a Scottish reel. Read the legend of *MacCodrum of the Seals* or *The Faery Flag of Dunvegan,* or any Scottish story.

GROUP ACTIVITIES
- **Bonfire Night posters:** Follow the discussion about safety on Bonfire Night by asking each group to design a poster to illustrate their most important rule. Use thick felt-tip pens or bubble writing for the letters. Keep the message simple or nobody will read it! Display all the posters in the entrance hall so that parents have an opportunity to see them.

- **Off to warmer lands:** Read 'Sky Arrows' by John Walsh. Why does the poet think that migrating birds look like arrows? Has anyone seen birds gathering on telephone wires or wheeling across the winter sky? What do they look like? (See Writing Activities.)

- Find out about birds which migrate (house martins, swallows, etc.) and those who over-winter here (robins, blackbirds, etc.). Draw or cut out pictures and place them in sets of migrating and non-migrating birds.

Migrating birds

Stay at home birds

- **Wild Creatures on the Doorstep:** Look out for wild creatures in parks, gardens - even in the playground. You might see squirrels, hedgehogs, bats or foxes. Wild birds are our most frequent visitors, so it is well worth constructing a bird table and putting out food (fat, nuts, sultanas, stale bread). Use bird books for identification and note the different birds who visit. Keep a class diary. Consider ways we can help wild creatures to survive in winter-time.

The Woods in Winter

● Make *Bat Watch, Bird Watch, Hedgehog Watch,* etc. badges for different groups. Make a collection of poems, pictures, stories and interesting facts about each particular creature.

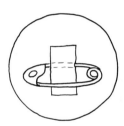

● **St Andrew's Day:** Make shortbread for St. Andrew's Day and decorate the classroom with Scottish flags and blue and white balloons or streamers.

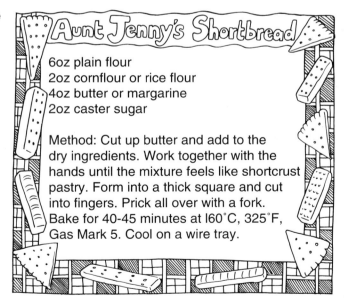

Aunt Jenny's Shortbread

6oz plain flour
2oz cornflour or rice flour
4oz butter or margarine
2oz caster sugar

Method: Cut up butter and add to the dry ingredients. Work together with the hands until the mixture feels like shortcrust pastry. Form into a thick square and cut into fingers. Prick all over with a fork. Bake for 40-45 minutes at 160°C, 325°F, Gas Mark 5. Cool on a wire tray.

● **November colour:** Read John Foster's poem 'November'. What is the colour he uses most often? Is he right, do you think? The poet says:
> November is a grey road
> Cloaked in mist.................

● Look at the weather - mostly cold, cloudy and grey, often raining, sometimes foggy. Even when the sun does shine, it is a pale silvery white. The colour has gone from the gardens, leaving sad-looking grass and bare earth. Choose a list of November colours. Make a colour wheel or a colour ladder.

- Leafless trees begin to show their bones; cow parsley, teazels and ferns become skeletons, and 'Old Man's Beard' tumbles over the hedgerows. Use this month to begin to identify trees by shape alone. Copy the outlines, using black pen. Gather dried cow parsley and teazels from the roadside and make a November display of skeleton and shape. (See photograph on page 19.)

- **Television review:** When the evenings are dark we are more likely to have time to watch television or videos. Talk about the programmes you enjoy watching, and choose the funniest, the most exciting, the spookiest. Choose one that made you feel sad or angry. Choose one that made you want to find out more.

- Get together in a group where you have all recently watched the same programme or video and each write a review.

    The programme was called..............
    It made me feel...............
    The character I liked best was. ....
    The best thing that happened was...............
    If I could have changed the ending, this is what would
        have happened...............

    Did you all think the same thing? Perhaps it sounds as if you all watched a different programme! Why?

- **Seeds from the Forest:** Look for conkers, the winged 'keys' of the ash tree, acorns and beechmast. Late autumn or early winter is the best time to collect tree seeds for growing on later into baby trees or *bonsais*. By this time they will be fully ripe. All tree seeds need to lie dormant for a couple of months, so store them in a cool place until the end of December, then plant them into a pot of compost or damp sand - not too deep - and place outdoors, out of the way of hungry birds or field mice. The next stage takes place in early spring.

WRITING ACTIVITIES
- **Planting seeds:** Collect and plant seeds as suggested in *Seeds from the Forest* above. Imagine that you meet a Woodman from Outer Space who has never seen an earthly tree. Write out instructions for finding conkers (what they look like, colour and shape, how they feel). You will need to describe a chestnut tree in detail, adding a sketch to help the Spaceman in his search. Then list five steps for planting the conkers. Make your description very clear and detailed.

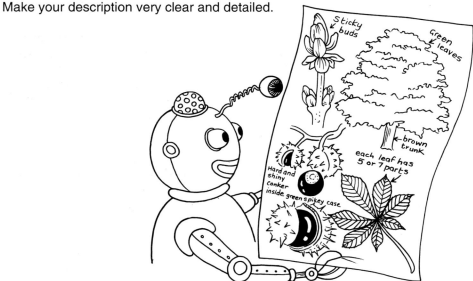

- **November is... :** Read John Foster's poem 'November'. Make a list of things about the month of November and list them in a similar way to John Foster. Give each idea two lines, so that the poem looks like this:

    November is skeleton trees
    pointing their fingers to the sky,
    It is a dark curtain closing
    in the early afternoon.
    November is....................
        ....

● **The Moon:** Read Moira Andrew's poem 'Autumn Sorrow'. Talk about the image she has used to describe the moon. How do you think she feels about late autumn? Can you turn her poem into a happy one? Call it 'Winter happiness'.

● List other images for the moon: toys - hoop, balloon, ball; jewels - crown, giant pearl, gold earring; food - cheese, pancake, banana. Think about what those things might do or how they would move. Take one line to suggest what the moon looks like, a second line to say what it does. Make your ideas into an image poem. (With the youngest children, use the first line of each couplet only.)

The moon is like a silver balloon
floating in the night sky.
It is like a golden crown
glittering on black velvet.

Use a silver pen to write your poem on black card with a silver-foil moon shape (see photograph).

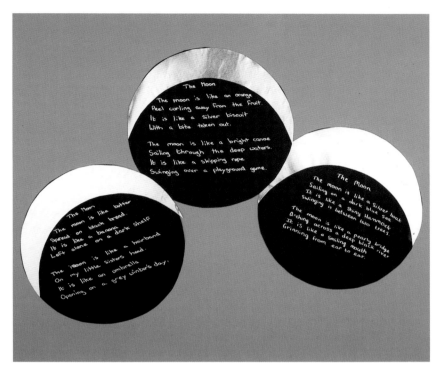

● **Sharing our lives:** Write letters to penfriends (real or imagined) in Australia, where November means summer, to children in Canada or Norway where the winters are colder than ours. Tell something about your own life, school, home, family, what you wear, what makes you laugh. (See *Talking Together*). Tell your penfriends what our November weather is like, the colours, the rain, the cold, the frost. Set your letter out correctly with your address or the school address (postcode included) and the date in the top right-hand corner. Try it out in rough first, then write in best or use the word processor. You could include a November poem in your letter.

● **Bonfire Night:** Read Ian Souter's poem 'Bonfire Night Lights'. Look for the movement words which he has used - *whoosh, splatter, race*. Find more movement words which could be used for a volcano, e.g. flow, erupt, gush, swirl, surge. Now use these volcano words in your own description of the fireworks as they flare up into the night sky. They should help to make the writing vivid and very exciting.

● Write a shape poem showing a flaring bonfire. Make the flames into fire-words, printing them in red, orange and yellow letters. Show fireworks exploding like the *WHOOSH!* in Ian Souter's poem.

● Read 'Fireworks' by Moira Andrew. She has used an image of flowers to describe the fireworks. Can you think of a different image? falling leaves? a waterfall? a fountain? Look closely at the way fireworks explode into the night and write a haiku, keeping your own image going throughout. A haiku has only three lines and you need to count the syllables or beats in each line. It has a 5 - 7 - 5 pattern, like this:

Firework fountain

Gushing and splashing   (5)
in showers of silver spray   (7)
night-time waterfall   (5)

● **Migrating birds:** Look at the way birds gather on telephone wires or fence posts. Listen to the noises they make. Imagine that you are the leading bird, planning to take your flock far away to the hot plains of Africa. Look up an atlas and trace the route that you must take. Can you work out what you will say to the youngsters who have never before made the journey? Work with a group to write out a set of instructions. You might say:

> *Following the bird in front.*
> *Never...............................*
> *Turn left when you see........................*
> *Always............................*
> *If you get tired....................................*

Think of at least ten rules and directions to get you
and the young birds safely from here to Africa.

Make a Bon Voyage card for a swallow on migration for the first time

● Look at the shape made by the birds in the 'Sky Arrows' poem and write your own short piece about birds getting ready to fly off to warmer lands. Use a different idea for your shape poem. (You might think that birds on telephone wires look like black notes on a music score!)

ART ACTIVITIES
● **Bonfire Night:** Read Ian Souter's poem 'Bonfire Night Lights' and 'Fireworks' by Moira Andrew. Find the words the poets use to express colour and movement. Look, listen, imagine taking part in a Guy Fawkes party outside. Think of the blackness of the night sky, of the *silver and blue, red and gold* of the fireworks.
● Use black cartridge paper, bright coloured inks or runny paint, and plastic straws to make a most effective firework picture. Put some ink or paint on the black paper and use the straws to blow colour across it. (Use lots of newspaper to cover the desk.) Scatter bright spark patterns into the night sky.
● Make a bonfire picture using red, yellow, orange tissue paper torn into flame shapes. Paste the tissue paper flat, overlaying colour on colour. Add one or two flames in blue, silver and gold - not too many - to give the fire more depth. Put a cut-out Guy on top as a silhouette.
● Make individual firework pictures by using a scraper-board technique. Fill a sheet of black card very densely with thick wax colour in yellow, red and orange. Then cover completely with black wax crayon. Scrape away the black with a penknife and a bright firework pattern will be revealed.

● **In Flanders Fields...:** Look at pictures of poppies and examine Remembrance Day poppies. Ask each child to paint his/her own poppy, making the petals the brightest red they can mix, and adding a dense black centre. (Try to make sure that there is a range of sizes.) When the pictures are dry, cut out and paste them *row on row,* small flowers in the background, larger ones in the front. To make this frieze really effective, use masses of poppies, in a range of reds individually mixed. You may like to add a few small white crosses among the flowers.

December

Christmas is ....
a fir tree
alone in a room corner,
patiently waiting
for its Christmas clothing.

snow outside
drifting to the ground.
Cotton wool padding
waiting to be torn apart.

Christmas Eve,
one single star.
A silver medal
hanging on an ebony neck.

Christmas morning,
waiting downstairs,
colourful Jack-in-the-boxes
ready to jump up in surprise!
Ian Souter

24 windows on the Advent calendar
A silver ball
A golden drum
Bright red crackers
Shiny apples
Holly berries
Four jingle bells
    And a robin
Green striped sweets
Fairy doll
Santa Claus
Candle light
Christmas tree
Three angels
    And a pudding
Snowman
Balloons
Choir girls
Turkey
Reindeer
    And a stocking
Star
King
Gifts
    AND A MANGER!
Rita Ray

The Christmas star
A star looked down
from the frosty sky,
saw three lost kings
and winked its eye.

'Follow me,' it said
and blazed a trail
over sand and plain,
up-hill, down-dale.

It stopped at Bethlehem
above a poor shed.
'Sure?' asked the kings,
'This child has no bed.'

'Sure,' said the star
and faded from sight,
as sun bathed the baby
in clear morning light.
Moira Andrew

Don't forget the birds

A hungry robin
looked for food
In Laura's frosty garden,
bobbed in a fir tree
underneath the eave,

Found that the branches
were full of surprises;
'An apple, nuts,
a coconut,
They must be make-believe!'

'Eat up!'
chirped a bluetit
hopped up beside him.
'Laura has remembered us.
Today is Christmas Eve!'
Irene Rawnsley

December's dawn
The sun gazes down
    from a Cyclops eye
at the dragon of winter
    feathering the fields
with its cold white breath.
Moira Andrew

TALKING TOGETHER

● **Christmas:** At this time of the year everything builds up to Christmas, so take the opportunity to approach the Christmas story from a number of different angles. Talk about the anonymous onlookers - shepherd boys on the hillside, children running around the yard outside the stable, servant lads attending the kings - what did these children think about the arrival of the special baby? Would they have brought gifts? If so, what kind of things might they have brought? Discuss why we like to give presents for birthdays, new babies, Christmas.

● **Road to Bethlehem:** Look at maps of the Bible lands. Think of the long hard road Mary and Joseph had to travel. Talk about paying taxes. What taxes do people pay now? What is the money used for? Discuss with the class how they would like to see the money raised from taxes used - homeless people, animal welfare, more buses, better playgrounds? In groups, make notes. Design a poster, using cut-out newspaper photographs alongside their own printed headlines. Perhaps older children might write about their ideas to local papers or to councillors.

● **Advent:** Talk about how parents, older brothers and sisters look forward to the birth of a new baby. Talk about the preparations they make - getting clothes ready, etc. Tell the children about the meaning of Advent, looking forward to the coming of Jesus.

● Make an Advent wreath using brightly covered P.E. hoops. Decorate with holly and tinsel. Add four candles, one to be lit each week in the four weeks before Christmas.

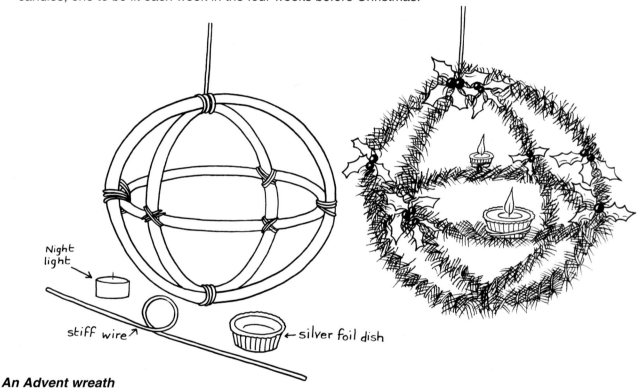

Night light

stiff wire ↗

silver foil dish →

An Advent wreath

● Read Rita Ray's poem '24 Windows on the Advent Calendar' and discuss different ways of making Advent calendars. (See Art Activities.) Let each group choose 24 Christmas pictures which they would like to use. Talk about reasons for their choices.

ASSEMBLIES

● **Christingle service:** The Christingle service can be one of the most effective and memorable of the Christmas assemblies. Each child has an orange, representing the world. Press a candle into the orange and tie a red ribbon round it. Let children walk into the church singing a familiar carol, each carrying a lighted Christingle to represent Jesus bringing light to the world.

● **Chanukkah or Hanukkah:** Chanukkah is the Jewish festival of light. On each of the eight days of the festival a candle is lit at sunset, both in the synagogue and at home. It is a happy time with prayers and presents, music and dancing. (The festival begins on a date between 28th November and 27th December.) Celebrate by lighting a candle over eight assemblies. Draw or paint an eight-branched candlestick (Menorah), adding a red and yellow flame-shape each day; or the outline of a house with eight windows, painting one window in gold on each day of the festival.

Surprise boxes - see below

● **Baboushka:** Tell the Baboushka legend. It casts an unfamiliar light on the traditional Christmas story.
Baboushka was a Russian woman who lived deep in the forest. One winter's night she piled up her log fire, baked cakes, made mulled wine and invited all her friends to join her in a feast.
While the party was taking place, shepherds saw a star and followed it. They stopped by Baboushka's cottage and asked her to go with them to find a new-born baby in a manger, but Baboushka was too busy entertaining her friends.
When the friends had gone, the house grew cold. One by one three kings knocked at Baboushka's door asking for food and rest. They invited her to go with them to follow the star and find the child that was to be born. Baboushka was too busy, too tired and she had no gift for the baby.
The shepherds and the kings met at the end of the forest and decided to travel together. They came to the stable and found Mary and Joseph and the baby Jesus.
When Baboushka woke up she was sad and disappointed that she had not journeyed to see the new baby, so she set off with a gift of holly, picked from the forest. But Baboushka was too late. Mary and Joseph and the baby had fled from Herod. Every star and every sign had gone. She searched for weeks and months and years. The legend says that she is searching still. At Christmas time, it is said, Baboushka still wraps up little gifts, leaving them for all the babies and young children she knows, always hoping that one day she will find the Christchild.

● Encourage children to write and perform a nativity play centred round the legend of Baboushka. Have a group - Baboushka's visitors - dressed in Russian costume, playing and dancing to folk music with the rest of the cast taking traditional roles.

GROUP ACTIVITIES
● **Birds' Christmas Tree:** Read Irene Rawnsley's poem 'Don't forget the birds' and 'December's Dawn' by Moira Andrew. What is *'the dragon of winter'*? Read bird books to find out what foods birds appreciate at this time of year when fields are feathered with the dragon's *'cold white breath'*. If there is an accessible bare-branched tree in the school grounds, hang food to make *'the branches full of surprises'* for the birds. Make a chart to record visitors to the Birds' Christmas Tree. (See Art Activities.)
● **Surprise Boxes:** Ask children to bring a selection of small boxes. Make a display of the boxes (see photograph above). What are the boxes made of? Look at shapes and colours. Rattle the boxes - full or empty? Smell inside - pot-pourri, dust, perfume? (See Writing Activities.)

- **The Christmas Star:** Read 'The Christmas Star'. The star has a conversation with the kings. Think about other people in the Christmas story who might have talked with the star - angels, shepherds, inn-keeper's children. Let each group choose people to talk with the star. Work out some questions and answers. Make them into a television/radio programme: 'Interviews with the Christmas Star'.
- Look for maps of the stars. Find out names of some of the constellations and make a star map for the wall.

WRITING ACTIVITIES

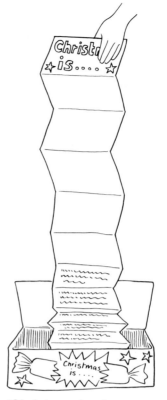

- **How many stars?:** This provides a simple pattern for the youngest children to follow:
    How many stars are shining
    on Christmas Day, on Christmas Day?
    Seven bright stars shining
    On Christmas Day in the morning.
    How many shepherds watching
    on Christmas Day, on Christmas Day?
    Six tired shepherds watching,
    Seven bright stars shining
    on Christmas Day in the morning.
And so on, until the children arrive at *One special baby leeping.*

- **Christmas is... :** Read Ian Souter's list poem 'Christmas is...'. Ask children to make up a list of people, weather, games, food - everything that Christmas means to them. Put the list together so that it has a rhythm, and display the finished poem on a long strip of paper which folds away in a colourful Jack-in-the-box.

'Christmas is...'

- **Box of Dreams:** Take a small box from the box display (see Group Activities) and think about what it might contain if it were magic. It might be full of dreams, of nightmares, of wishes, of colours or sounds. Talk to your partner about it. Make up a poem, individually or with your partner, about the magic box.
    Inside the box of wishes
    where mists swirl and magic lurks
    lie dreams of rainbows, dreams of summer,
    dreams of ....
Imagine what might happen if the lid were suddenly closed, if the box were dropped, if a genie escaped....

- Another way of tackling the poem is to use a chorus:
    Open the box
    and what do I see?

- For the youngest child use a noun/adjective/verb pattern. Collect imagined 'magic' creatures: ant, spider, bee. Write their names down the *middle* of board or page. Add a colour on the left, a verb on the right, so that it looks like this:
    a golden ant marching
    a silver spider spinning
    a stripey bee buzzing...

'Top and tail' the poem, for example,
    Is it
    a golden ant marching?
    a silver spider spinning?

    We don't know, so
    let's open the lid and look!

● Display the magic/secret box poems inside an opening box (see photograph).

● Write about a magic Christmas parcel in the same way. Show the children a small beautifully-decorated parcel. Guess what's inside.

What's inside the Christmas parcel?
Is it
a red-nosed reindeer prancing?
a silver snowflake drifting?
a misty angel flying?
....

I feel it, I rattle it,
I turn it upside down.
How I wish that
Christmas morning
would hurry up and come!

● **The Christmas Story:** Listen to the Christmas story. Help the children write their own version edited into separate episodes. Make a 'peep-show' book with the story on one side of the page and each scene shown beneath a lift-up flap or within a decorative border.

● Tell the story in a comic strip, with speech bubbles.

- **Bethlehem Times:** Write and edit a newspaper bringing the story of the birth of Jesus. Try to cover the story in different ways: our Special Correspondent to write up the main event; our Royal Correspondent to write about the kings (what they wore, what gifts they brought); our Farming Correspondent to tell about the shepherds; our Astral Expert to give an account of the stars that night; our Woman's Page Editor to write about Mary and the baby - and so on. Perhaps the young people in the story got a bit bored with it all, so you might have a Sports Correspondent to report on a football match between the Shepherd Boys XI and the Local Lads XI!

ART ACTIVITIES

- **Advent calendars:** Read Rita Ray's poem. Use two matching sheets of thin card to make an Advent calendar with 24 opening windows. Cut round three sides of each window and inside draw a tiny picture of everything the poet suggests. Number the windows 1-24 and open one each day during Advent.
- Make a set of 24 stocking shapes (doubled) and hang on a string. Use felt-tip pens to colour them in bright stripey patterns. Number them and hide a small sweet inside each stocking.
- Make Advent Boxes to hang on ribbons. Cover 24 small boxes (match boxes would be ideal) in bright paper. Tie with coloured string and number them for each day of Advent. Fill with Smarties or Dolly Mixtures.

- **Christmas mobiles:** Make mobiles using a Christmas motif - tree, star, Father Christmas, snowman, etc. (see basic instructions on page 10). Decorate with scraps cut from old Christmas cards.

- Try a Nativity scene as a mobile. Use a stable shape for the frame, and set cut-outs of Mary and Joseph and the baby inside.

● **Winter mobile:** Read Irene Rawnsley's poem 'Don't forget the birds' and cut out a bare-branched tree. Using white card for maximum effect, follow basic instructions for mobile on page 10, but stretch clingfilm between the circles. Paste down and trim when dry. Use thick poster paint for falling snow.

● **'Stained-glass' windows:** On a sheet of top copy quality typing paper, draw a design or a Christmas scene heavily outlined in black wax crayon. Fill in the shapes between the black lines in bright 'jewel' colours, leaving no paper showing through. Turn your picture over and use cotton wool to rub the back of the paper with a little vegetable oil. The picture or pattern will look like stained glass if you fix it to the classroom window and let the light shine through.

● **The Christmas Story:** Make each group responsible for an episode in the Nativity story, and ask them to paint the figures on separate sheets of cartridge paper. Dry and cut out. Look at picture books to find out what the clothes were like. Use scraps of various fabric for robes and cloaks, plain blue for Mary, dull woollens for the shepherds, rich materials for the kings. Paste on to a prepared background with areas marked out for each scene. Fill in the spaces with massed fir trees, overlapping hills and a sky full of stars. (See page 4.)

● **Christmas tree decorations:** For unusual tree decorations, use salt dough (from the recipe on page 72). Make flat fir tree, star and candle shapes, either plain or painted in poster paints. For each new piece, e.g. the candle flame, use a new ball of dough, joining it to the main shape by using a pastry brush dipped in water. It is best to keep the dough in a polythene bag, taking out only as much as you need at a time. Work directly on to the baking tray. Make a hanger from fine twisted wire or a bent paperclip pushed into the dough.

January

Chinese New Year Dragon

There's a brightly coloured dragon swaying down the street,
Stomping and stamping and kicking up its feet.

There's a multi-coloured dragon - green, gold and red -
Twisting and twirling and shaking its head.

There's a silky-scaled dragon parading through the town,
Swishing and swooshing and rippling up and down.

There's a swirling, whirling dragon, weaving to and fro
Prancing and dancing and putting on a show.

There's cheering and clapping as the dragon draws near -
A sign of good luck and a happy new year.

John Foster

Snow Problem

You can't make friends with a snowman,
So don't give one a cuddle,
Or you'll end up
With a wet shirt front
Standing in a puddle.

John Coldwell

January

Trees traced in ink
with a fine-point nib,
fence posts stitched
to the sky, bleak days
wrapped in a shawl
and weeping.

(Part poem)
Moira Andrew

New Beginning

I won't come in late from school Mum
if you'll promise to give up smoking.
I'll try not to tease my sister,
She knows I'm only joking.

If you promise not to shout so much
I'll pick up my clothes at night,
just don't moan at me all day
and I'll keep away from fights.

Last year's new beginning
didn't last for very long.
I kept my part of the bargain Mum -
But where did you go wrong?

Brian Moses

TALKING TOGETHER

● **New Year Resolutions:** Read 'New Beginning' by Brian Moses. The turn of the year is the time to make lists of new ambitions, to think of ways of changing for the better, to resolve to try again. Discuss with the children how they might want to change their behaviour for the better, towards their parents perhaps, or towards one another. Talk about what is feasible. Let them work individually or in twos to write out a list of ten ways of improving their own lives - encourage them to suggest ideas that are both funny and serious, but all things that they could reasonably achieve. Make a set of small coloured envelopes, one for each child. Let them choose one resolution to seal inside their own envelope. (The teacher could do this too - all in secret!) Hang the envelopes on ribbons and make a tag reading 'Our New Year Resolutions'.

● **Weather Diary:** Begin a weather diary. Talk about different kinds of weather and look for unusual symbols which would best represent rain/cloud/fog/sunshine/snow, etc. An umbrella is the usual rain symbol, so think of something different, e.g. Wellington boots, duck, rainbow. Work out dates so that each group takes its turn to record the weather. Look for poems about weather and copy out for handwriting practice. Use the illustrated poems as part of the weather diaries. (Read John Coldwell's 'Snow Problem'.)

Chinese New Year Dragon, see page 35

- **Burns' Night:** Robert Burns, the Scottish poet, was born on 25th January, 1759. Look for poems by Burns and try to read them aloud. Think of the way Burns uses the Scots dialect and find other poems written in a different dialect, e.g. some of the work of John Agard, Grace Nichols, Benjamin Zephaniah. Try writing down a few phrases the children might use in their local 'street' dialect.
- Have a Burns' Night feast. Serve *chappit tatties* (mashed potatoes), and *neeps* (swede) with haggis as an optional extra - an acquired taste! Make *Aunt Jenny's Shortbread* (see November) for afters. Learn a Scottish reel and some Scots' folk songs. Burns' Night is an occasion for feasting and music. Say Burns' grace before the meal:
    Some ha'e meat, and canna eat,
    And some wad eat that want it;
    But we ha'e meat, and we can eat,
    And so the Lord be thankit. (Robert Burns)

- Make up a grace in the local dialect and use it before school lunch.

ASSEMBLIES
- **New beginnings:** At the first assembly of the new year, get the children to shake hands with those sitting either side, and wish each other 'A Happy New Year!' Read 'New Beginning' by Brian Moses. Talk about the opportunities a new year brings. It can be a time for getting rid of laziness or bad habits and resolving to change our ways. Suggest that each child makes *one* personal secret pact with him/herself. Take a minute's silence to think about it. Put on a quiet thought-provoking tape (e.g. Adagio from Mozart's 'Clarinet Concerto') and let the children walk quietly back to their classrooms, thinking - not talking.

- **Twelfth Night:** Twelfth Night falls on 6th January and is traditionally the date when Christmas decorations are taken down. It is also the day when the Christian Church celebrates the visit of the Three Wise Men to the stable. Think of the gifts that they brought to the baby Jesus - gold, frankincense and myrrh; gold to acknowledge that Jesus was the Son of God, frankincense for his work as a priest and myrrh to symbolise his suffering. Let three children, dressed as kings, bring new pound coins, an incense candle and some ointment. Talk about how and where these gifts might be used today. Sing the hymn 'We Three Kings of Orient are'.

- **Chinese New Year:** This colourful festival falls between 21st January and 19th February on the first day of the first month of the Chinese calendar. Talk about different ways of celebrating New Year - ringing church bells, setting off ships' sirens in the harbour, coloured lights in the streets; the Scottish custom of bringing presents of salt, coal and silver money (symbolising food, heat and wealth) to each house visited on the first day of the year. The Chinese celebrate their New Year first by cleaning the house from top to bottom, then by wearing new clothes, giving presents and putting fresh flowers in every room. Then they take to the streets dressed up as dragons. Read John Foster's 'Chinese New Year Dragon'.

- Decorate the hall with flags and banners, Chinese-style. Draw and paint pictures of the most colourful dragons you can imagine, *'green and gold and red'*. Make a dancing dragon (see Art Activities) and dance to Chinese music, *'swirling and whirling, prancing and dancing'* wishing a happy new year to everyone in the school as you dance along. Make it a very happy occasion.

GROUP ACTIVITIES

- **Snowman competition:** If it snows to any depth, make the most of it in school. Read John Coldwell's 'Snow Problem'. Work out a way in which you might indeed make friends with a snowman! (Think of *The Snowman* by Raymond Briggs.) Let the children have a snowman competition, giving each group minimum props, e.g. hat, scarf. Ask them to give their snowman a personality - happy, sad, cross - and to show it in the way they sculpt the face.

- Organise snow sculpture competitions. Get the children to make flowers and leaves, cactus plants, a beach scene - something connected with summer, not winter, for maximum effect. Don't forget to take photographs, as the sculptures won't last long.

- **Winter twigs:** Look at leafless trees and work on recognition simply from outline and shape. Winter is often the best time to study buds and branches. Take a twig and press it into clay or Plasticine. (Leave the end sticking out so that you can lift the twig away without spoiling the imprint.) You can use the clay impression to make a mould. Make a collar of card to fit around the clay. Oil the clay lightly by smearing with Vaseline, then pour in some plaster of Paris and leave overnight to set. Make casts from different kinds of twigs. Label them so that you can begin to recognise trees just from their winter shapes.

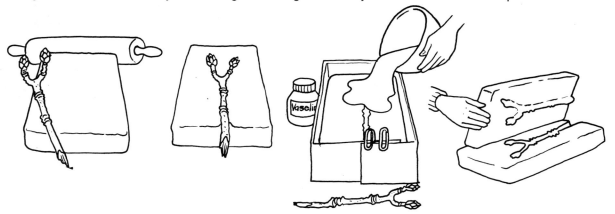

- Using the same method, you can make casts of fallen leaves, poppy heads, pine cones etc. You might make a winter plaque using a variety of found materials: feathers, shells, stones, evergreen leaves. Place them in a pleasing design, press into the clay and fill with plaster of Paris, as above.

- **Do birds have favourite colours?** You can make effective bird feeders from empty milk cartons. String them on wire and put some wild bird seed inside. To find out if the birds have favourite colours, paint each carton in a different colour and watch to see which one is visited most often.

- In the same way, you can record which foods birds like best when the ground is too hard for them to catch worms and grubs. Offer sultanas, fat, bread and wild bird seed. Record their likes and dislikes on a simple chart. Fill in the chart at lunchtime each day for a week.
- Don't forget to provide water for the birds, especially when there is frost and ice on the ground.

Your island's holiday brochure

Your own 'Island in the Sun'

WRITING ACTIVITIES

● **Island in the sun:** When the weather is bleak, *days wrapped in a shawl/and weeping* (January), it is a good time to plan summer holidays. Imagine your own island in the sun. Make a map of the island showing all the special features you would like it to have: palm trees, treasure chest, boating lake, waterfall, swimming pool. Make it as exotic as possible. (See photograph above.)

● Look at some holiday brochures and think of how you could advertise your island in the same way. Make a holiday brochure so that people reading it would really want to visit the island. (You might use the classroom word processor.) Illustrate with colourful pictures of hotels and apartments, sea and shore, amusement parks - even secret places where you can lie dreaming in the sun. Give prices for accommodation and information for travelling to your island in the sun.

● **New Beginnings:** Make a list of all the things you have done for the first time in the new year, e.g. opened the back door, looked out of the window, walked to the shops, listened to the birds, arrived at the school gate. Imagine that you have never done any of these things before and make a list poem beginning:

> I looked out of the window,
> for the first time, for the first time,
> I saw the sun shining on snow
> like..
> for the first time, for the first time

> I opened the door and walked out,
> for the first time, for the first time.........
> I saw/I heard ....

Follow the pattern, using the words *for the first time, for the first time,* as a chorus.

● **Snowman Diary:** Write your diary for a week as though you are a snowman. It might begin something like this:

Monday: Snow fell last night. I heard children laughing. I felt them build my body. I felt them make my head. They gave me eyes made of stones - I can see! I can see!

Go on from there, telling the snowman's own story. Tell what he sees, what he can hear, what he says. It might be sad at the end when the sun comes out and melts the snowman away, leaving only two stones, a carrot, some orange peel (what could that be used for?), a hat and a scarf. Make a zig-zag book, taking a page a day for your diary. You could cut it into the shape of a snowman. (See photograph.)

- **Winter trees:** Read Moira Andrew's poem 'January'. Why do you think she uses the idea that the trees are *traced in ink/with a fine-point nib?* Look closely at leafless trees. How else might you describe the way they look against a winter sky? Like *the caretaker's broom?* or *skeleton fingers?* Write a five line poem describing trees in winter. Remember to extend your original idea: if trees are like a broom, they might *sweep the sky clean.* If they are like skeleton fingers they might *point the way to night.*

- **Snow:** Think of what snow looks like, how it moves as it falls, think how it feels, how it might taste, how silent it is. Make a list of frail white things, always keeping the idea of snow in your mind. You might have thought of feathers, icing sugar, daisy petals. Write down at least eight ideas and use your list to make a poem.

  > Snow
  > Snow is like a dove's feathers
  > swirling from the clouds.
  > It is like skimmed milk
  > spilled on God's doorstep.

  The first line says what snow looks like, and the second says what it does or how it moves. Write two verses of four lines each. Use your most unusual ideas and scrap the rest.

- **Twelfth Night** (Epiphany): Tell the story of a Christmas tree from its time growing in the deep cold forest to hearing human footsteps and the sound of a saw. Tell how the tree feels as it is decorated with lights and stars, tinsel and baubles. Tell about heat and light and laughter. Finish your story on Twelfth Night when the tree is left bare. Is it a sad story? Perhaps your tree was dug up complete with roots and is planted in the back garden for the birds to nest in. Find your own ending, happy or sad. Make a book called 'The Little Christmas Tree'.

ART ACTIVITIES
- **Trees traced in ink:** Read Moira Andrew's 'January'. Look at the shapes of leafless trees. Using a 'sgraffito' (scraped crayons) technique, fill a sheet of strong black card with thick white wax crayon. Use a penknife to scrape the outlines of winter trees in black on white, making a winter landscape against the snow.

- **Calendars:** Look at calendars and diaries. Work out a plan for making a calendar for yourself. It might be in a zig-zag shape, using six pages (back and front) with dates copied from this year's diary. You might make a calendar which opens to a new sheet for each month. Find or draw a picture for each month and copy days and dates beneath the picture. You might design a loose-leaf calendar which opens like a diary and has room for writing notes.

- Make a 'poetry calendar' with a simple picture and a poem which you have either copied or written to suit each month. This makes an excellent New Year's gift.

- **Snow Problem:** Read John Coldwell's poem. Draw a snowman, snowflakes falling, snow on the ground etc., using a white candle or white wax crayon on white paper. Reveal the 'hidden' picture by brushing a thin coat of blue watercolour paint over the picture in wax relief style.

- **Chinese Dragon:** Using John Foster's poem 'Chinese New Year Dragon' as a basis, let a number of children join forces to become *a brightly coloured dragon*. Give each child a tabard made from a plastic carrier bag (simply cut open the bottom of the bag and wear over the shoulders by the handle loops). Decorate the tabards with fringes of contrasting tissue or crêpe paper sewn, taped or stapled from the lower hem upwards. Make a dragon mask from card for the child at the head of the dragon, and a long dragging tail for the one at the back. Each child might wear a bright paper cap. They hold each other conga-style and make up a dragon dance, *Stomping and stamping and kicking....*

- Use collage materials, or overlapped tissue paper, to make a *multi-coloured dragon* dancing along the street; or paint one, each child painting and cutting out a section of the body. Give the dragon fierce flames made from red, yellow and orange tissue paper layered over and over. (See photograph on page 3l.)

- Make kites from paper or plastic carrier bags to help celebrate the Chinese New Year. Paint the bags in bright poster colours and decorate with bold patterns. Fold over the top edge of the bag and tape to make it double thickness. Punch four holes spaced evenly apart in the double-thickness and about 4cm from the edge. Put reinforcement rings on both side of the hole. Now cut two lengths of string to the loops to make a handle. Glue on coloured streamers cut from crepe paper or foil. Open the bag, hold tight to the handle and run with your kite in the wind.

- **Snowman mobile:** Make the mobile using basic instructions on page 10, but stretch clingfilm over one circle before attaching the other. Glue together and trim the clingfilm when dry. Snow is made with thick poster paint dabbed onto the clingfilm.

February

Magpie world

Outside this morning
everything's white.
There's been a hoar-frost
overnight.

The trees are dark
against the sky,
the fields are glittering
bright with ice.

Four rooks flap by
in this magpie world
the sun pale shining,
yellow pearl

Joan Poulson

Winter window

Frosted fairies, powder-light,
feathered their tiny wings, last night,
across my winter window,

carved a crystal paradise
of snowflake patterns and bracken, in ice,
across my winter window,

blew cold, rolling scrolls and curls
that froze to etch an Arctic world
across my winter window.

Gina Douthwaite

Snow-stroll

I
love
the
snow
I
love
the
cold
I
love
the
crispy
patterns
my
feet
leave
behind
I
love
the
crunchy
sound
they
make
as
I
stroll
along
changing
direction
again
and
again
and
a
g
a
i
n

John Walsh

TALKING TOGETHER

- **Candlemass:** Candlemass, the Festival of Candles, is held on 2nd February and celebrates the day that the infant Jesus was first brought to the temple by his mother.
- Talk about what happens at christening services. Look at christening photographs. Make a table display of baby clothes, showing a christening robe, if possible. Add photographs of the children as babies and have a 'Who's who?' guessing game.
- Talk about using candles today - in church, on birthday cakes, at Christmas time, when the electricity fails. Light a candle and watch the way the flame flickers. Put the lights out and close the blinds. Think about the light from one candle. Imagine what it was like before electricity was invented. Talk about going to bed by candlelight, shadows on the wall, trying to read.

Mardi Gras masks, see page 40

● Look closely at the weather on 2nd February. There is an old country saying that goes like this:
    If Candlemass be fine and clear
    There'll be two winters in that year.
Talk about what this means. Do you think there is any truth in it? If there is, what kind of weather will this year hold? Find other country weather sayings. Write them out in your weather notebook and illustrate them. You might be able to find out if any of them come true!

● **Winter world:** On a day of frost, read Gina Douthwaite's poem 'Winter Window'. Find winter words in the poem. Talk about how frost changes the look of familiar things - how it whitens fences and branches. Talk about snow, wind, fog. What changes do they make to the things we see around us?

● Read 'Magpie World' by Joan Poulson. Why do you think the poet has chosen this particular title? Talk about things that are always black and white - chessboard, penguin, newspaper, etc. - and suggest other titles for Joan Poulson's poem. Have a competition to see how many different titles you can find. Make a black and white display.
● Talk about warm colours and cold colours. Make colour wheels for hot and cold.

● **St Valentine's Day:** I4th February is a day which causes much excitement - even among primary school children! Remind the children that cards and messages should be anonymous. Suggest sending notes to mums, dads or grandparents (especially those living alone) to say how much they love them.
● There is a tradition that birds choose their mates on St Valentine's Day, so it can be interesting to think about the kind of message a bird might send. Design Valentine cards for the birds.

ASSEMBLIES
● **Candlemass:** Have a candle festival using as many different kinds of candles as possible. Look at the way a single candle flame can light up the darkness and think about why Jesus was called *the Light of the World.*
● **Winter weather:** Think about how we protect ourselves from the cold - clothes, warm food, shelter, heating. Think about others, especially children, who are not so lucky. It might be an opportunity to make a collection of good outgrown clothing to be sent to less fortunate places across the world. Invite people from Oxfam or some other charity to talk to the children about their work overseas.
● **Ash Wednesday:** Ash Wednesday is the first day of Lent, the forty days leading up to Easter. Christians regard Ash Wednesday as one of the holiest days of the year. It is a day to think of how Jesus came to work among us on earth.

- Read stories about Jesus spending forty days alone in the wilderness. Talk about how many Christians remember this by giving up something they really enjoy for Lent. Some may give to charity, some may spend more time in worship. Discuss with the children what they would find hardest to give up, and why.

GROUP ACTIVITIES
- **Shrove Tuesday (Pancake Day):** Shrove Tuesday (between 3rd February and 9th March) is the day before Ash Wednesday. At one time many people fasted during Lent, so they tried to use up all the rich food in the house, and pancakes were a good way of using eggs and butter.
- Make pancakes and invite parents or the kitchen staff to share them. Print lemon-shaped invitations. Decorate the tables in green and yellow to welcome spring. Put lemon slices and sugar ready.

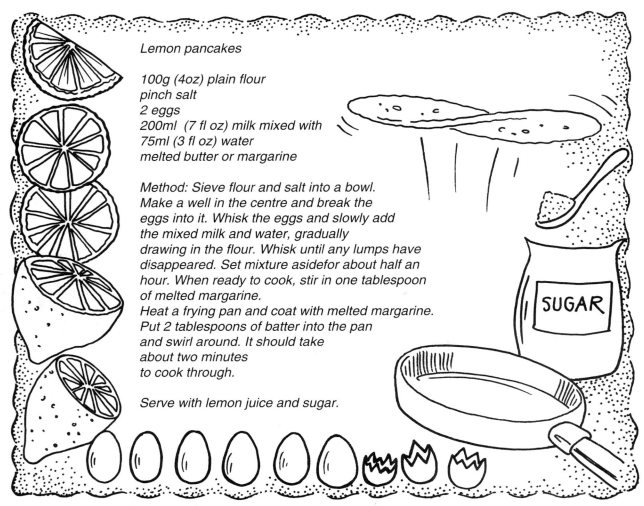

Lemon pancakes

100g (4oz) plain flour
pinch salt
2 eggs
200ml (7 fl oz) milk mixed with
75ml (3 fl oz) water
melted butter or margarine

Method: Sieve flour and salt into a bowl. Make a well in the centre and break the eggs into it. Whisk the eggs and slowly add the mixed milk and water, gradually drawing in the flour. Whisk until any lumps have disappeared. Set mixture aside for about half an hour. When ready to cook, stir in one tablespoon of melted margarine.
Heat a frying pan and coat with melted margarine. Put 2 tablespoons of batter into the pan and swirl around. It should take about two minutes to cook through.

Serve with lemon juice and sugar.

- **Mardi Gras:** This is the French name for Shrove Tuesday. In European countries the festival is celebrated with grand outdoor parades, music and dancing. In the Caribbean tradition, revellers wear colourful masks when they dance.

- Organise a Mardi Gras carnival to cheer up a cold February day. Let the children dress up in their brightest clothes and dance to Calypso music. Encourage them to make and decorate masks for the carnival. Simple masks can be made from the backs of cereal packets, more complicated ones using papier mâché. (See Art Activities.) The Mardi Gras carnival could be part of a larger Arts Festival of story and poetry, music and dance, art and drama. Invite professional artists to take part and involve all the children and their parents. (Arts grants are often available from the Arts Council.)

- **Candlemass:** Try science experiments using candles. Write up the results in your science notebook.
- Find out what happens when a lit candle is deprived of air.
- Make candle clocks.
- Use a white candle on white paper to send a secret message. Wash over with a thin coat of water colour paint to reveal the message. Think about how this happens.

● **Animal tracks:** If snow has fallen overnight, it might be possible to work out which animals or birds have visited the school grounds. Soft newly-fallen snow makes the tracks stand out. Look for signs of cats and dogs, rabbits, squirrels, foxes or hedgehogs. Check the prints from an animal book. Record the tracks in your nature notebooks. You can trace prints by using a black felt-tip pen on a clear plastic sheet or OHP transparency.

● Read 'Snow-stroll' by John Walsh. Look at the pattern the poet has made with the words. Why do you think he has arranged them in this way? Use a plan of the school grounds and let each group mark out a pattern in the style of 'taking a line for a walk'. Try to walk across the snow, making footsteps like the pattern on the page.

WRITING ACTIVITIES

● **Winter windows:** When there has been an overnight frost, let the children look out of the window. List all the changes in the familiar environment. Read Gina Douthwaite's poem 'Winter Window'. From your list of ideas, put a copycat poem together using her pattern. You might end each verse, as the poet does, with the phrase *'across (or through or from) my winter window'*. Display your poem in an open window frame, using clingfilm for the glass. (See photograph.)

● **Recipe for winter:** Think of what is special about winter and make three lists: winter weather, what you can see from the window, games you like to play. You need about four ideas in each list. Now put your thoughts into a winter poem using a recipe pattern. It might look like this:

> *Take some deep soft snow,*
> *an ice-covered pond*
> *and ....*
> **Add** *(choose three things from the 'what I can see' list)*
> **Mix with** *(choose three wintertime games)*
> **Decorate with** *frost as white as lace,*
> *some sparkling morning sun*
> *and keep at the back of the freezer.*

To make an effective poem, use recipe commands (*Add, Mix, Stir, Whisk etc.*) and make each verse just three lines long. (See photograph.)

- **On a cold and frosty morning:** This is a writing idea growing from feelings about the cold. Begin from the Candlemass rhyme (See Talking Together) and gather cold weather words. Let children suggest ideas and put them in a word wheel. Talk about where the coldest place in the world might be - at the South Pole? inside a bag of frozen peas? in the heart of a snowman?

- Write a story or a poem from the coldest place you can imagine, using all the *bitter, freezing, perishing* words in your vocabulary. When your stories and poems are finished, read them aloud and give an icicle-shaped medal to the author whose work really made people shiver with cold!

- **Valentine poems:** Write short poems, no more than five lines, to say *I love you*. Make them funny or serious, but keep them anonymous (for the teacher's eyes only, perhaps?). Put them on cut-out red hearts and hang them from a Valentine tree. (See Art Activities.)

- **Walking in the snow:** Read 'Snow-stroll' and go out in the snow. Feel how your boots make marks, listen to the crunch, look at the footprints you leave behind. Once back in the classroom, write about walking in the snow. Let your words make a pattern on the page in the same kind of way that John Walsh has done.

- **Here I discovered snow:** Imagine that you are newly arrived from a land of sunshine where snow is only seen in picture books. Imagine the day that you first discover snow. Write a diary page telling how beautiful snow looks, how silently it falls, how you can't wait to get outside. Are you pleased or disappointed?

- **Imagine a world without colour:** Read Joan Poulson's 'Magpie World'. The poet says that outside everything is white, except for bare trees and a few rooks. Imagine how the world would be changed if there were no colour, if everything were in shades of black and white. Imagine black flowers against a white sky. Look at old photographs to see what things would look like. Make up a questionnaire to find out what people would miss most. Use the answers to write a story about the black and white world of an old photograph.

- **Talking Masks:** With the Mardi Gras masks, use the 'hot seat' idea to question some of the characters about where they come from, their favourite food, how they feel about school, etc. Make the answers into a conversation piece between two characters.
    Moonman: I live on the mountains of the moon.
    Dragon: I live in caves deep inside a volcano.
    Moonman: My father has the voice of an angel.
    Dragon: My father has the voice of a thunderstorm.
This piece might develop into a bit of wild boasting - or into a lasting friendship. Let the children hide behind the masks and invent new identities and fantastic lifestyles.

ART ACTIVITIES
- **Winter twigs:** Cut a bare twig with an unopened bud (Horse Chestnut is best). Put the twig in water and watch the bud unfold in the heat. Draw what you see happening to the twig, from bud through to leaf. (See title page.) and keep a record of the date. Paste the drawings in your nature notebook.

- **Candle patterns:** Use candles or wax crayons to make wax resist patterns. Make a winter scene: bare trees, fences, snowmen (or make a series of snowflake patterns), using a white candle or wax crayons on white paper. Wash over with a thin layer of pale blue watercolour, and a cold-looking winter picture will emerge.

- **Through the window:** Make winter window mobiles. Make a rough sketch of the scene, cutting out unnecessary details, and draw the outline inside your window shape. Use stretched clingfilm for the glass. Hang from a thread. (See photograph on page 2.)

- **Mardi Gras masks:** Use the backs of cereal packets or thin card to make simple masks for infant children. Tape the masks on to old rulers or sticks as some young children do not like the sensation of being trapped inside a mask. Make the faces very colourful using poster paint, tissue paper or wool for hair, with feathers or beads just for fun! (See photograph on page 37.)

- Make a fearsome monster mask by cutting out a spiky shape from card. Cover the shape with black drawing ink or black poster paint. When it is dry, draw thick warrior-like patterns on it, using bright wax crayons. You need to press very hard. Using a cocktail stick, scratch out black line patterns on the coloured wax.
  Make holes at the sides and tie the masks on with string or elastic.

- Make papier mâché masks on balloons. Blow up the balloon and rub it over with petroleum jelly. Now cover with strips of torn newspaper alternating with flour paste until you have several layers. Let the papier mâché dry out. Pop the balloon and carefully cut the 'head' in two, to give you two masks. Paint and decorate using thick poster colours.

- More elaborate moulded masks can be made using a clay block. Mould the face with nose and eyes in clay. Cover the clay closely with clingfilm and let it dry out. Build up layers of papier mâché, using torn newsprint and flour paste. When the mask is dry, remove it from the clay mould and decorate with poster paint and scraps of wool or strips of cloth for hair.

- **Magpie world:** Read Joan Poulson's poem and make a black and white picture using wax resist (black trees in a white world) or sgraffito (scraper board) technique.

- **Valentine cards:** Make a range of Valentine cards, from simple folded cards to pop-ups. Make Valentine mobiles inside a heart shape, using basic instructions on page 10.

- **Valentine tree:** Make a tall tree in outline using cut black or dark brown sugar paper. Cut out red hearts in card and let the children print Valentine poems on them. Make a hole and thread red wool or cotton through it. Hang the poem hearts on the tree. (See Writing Activities.)

March

Windy Playground

They played blow-me-down in the yard,
letting the wind bully them,
coats above heads, arms spread wide,
daring the wind to do its worst.
They leant forward against the blow
as it rallied and flung them back
then coats puffed out like clouds
they returned to attack the blast,
while the gale drew a breath and then
pressed relentless. Till wild in defeat
and magnificent, they grouped again
and stretched their wings, stubborn
as early airmen.

Brian Moses

Mad March Sun

Woods were waking up today
after the snow.
Twigs stretched away winter stiffness,
ticked dry
in the mad March sun.

Mists rolled along ribbed fields
warmed from wetness
to dress a threadbare hedge
as black scraps of boasting crows
called taunts across the sky's playground.

Gina Douthwaite

It's spring

It's spring
And the garden is changing its clothes
Putting away
Its dark winter suits,
Its dull scarves
And drab brown overcoats.

Now, it wraps itself in green shoots
Slips on blouses
Sleeved with pink and white blossom,
Pulls on skirts of daffodil and primrose,
Snowdrop socks and purple crocus shoes,
Then dances in the sunlight.

John Foster

Portrait of a Dragon

If I were an artist
I'd paint the portrait
    of a dragon.

To do a proper job
I'd borrow colours
    from the world.

For his back I'd
need a mountain range,
    all misty blue.

For spikes, I'd use
dark fir trees pointing
    to the sky.

For overlapping scales
I'd squeeze dye from
    bright anemones.

I'd gild his claws
like shining swords
    with starlight.

His tail would be
a river, silver
    in the sun.

For his head, the
secret green of forests
    and deep seas.

And his eyes would
glow like embers in
    a tinker's fire.

But I'd keep the best
till last. For his
    hot breath

I'd use all reds and
yellows - crocus, saffron,
    peony, poppy,

geranium, cyclamen, rose -
and fierce orange flames
    from a marigold.

Moira Andrew

● **Easter eggs:** Ask children each to bring in a hard-boiled egg. Using thick wax crayons, draw a zig-zag design on the egg. Make up some fabric dye or undiluted food colouring for the egg, making sure that it is completely covered. Check the depth of colour from time to time. When it is the colour you want, lift the egg out and let it dry on clingfilm or crumpled foil. Don't use eggs which have cracked in the pan.

TALKING TOGETHER
● **St David's Day:** St David's Day is celebrated on lst March. On that day, the people of Wales wear the national emblems of leek or daffodil in honour of their patron saint. Another favourite Welsh symbol is the dragon. Look for Wales on a map of the world, or the United Kingdom. Is there anyone who can speak Welsh?
● Talk about ancestors and where they come from. This can lead to some interesting discussion. Are there children whose parents come from other parts of the United Kingdom, or from abroad? Talk about different traditions and languages which come together to make a richer pattern of life.
● Find stories, poems and legends about dragons. Make a table display of dragon books and pictures.

● **St Patrick's Day:** The Irish celebrate their national saint's day on 17th March, and on that day they wear the shamrock, the national symbol of Ireland. Talk about the Celts in Britain: Irish, Welsh, Scots and the people of Cornwall, all of whom feel a special identity. Talk about their music and legends.

● **March winds:** March is notorious for its high winds. When the wind blows, read 'Windy Playground' by Brian Moses. Watch what happens to trees in a high wind, to long grass, to litter left lying about. Talk about how the wind itself is invisible, although you can feel it and see the effect it has on things around us.
● Talk about the senses with which you can experience wind. Can wind be tasted? Think of salt winds by the sea.
● Talk about what it must be like to be invisible. Are there are other things which can be felt and heard, but can't be seen? Talk about music - you can hear it, of course, but can you feel music? Try 'listening' with your fingers to the beat of a drum. The discussion might lead to talk about spirits and ghosts.

ASSEMBLIES
● **St David's Day:** There is an interesting and little known legend about St David which closely parallels the story of Jesus. One night the king of Wales dreamed that an angel brought news of a special baby that was soon to be born. He told the king that the baby would grow up to be very powerful and wise.
The king, who did not want anyone to be more powerful than himself, ordered his soldiers to kill every new-born boy baby in the kingdom. The mothers heard about this and tried to hide their babies in caves and under bushes. One night there was such a fierce storm that the soldiers were forced to shelter and on that very night St David was born.
St David grew up to be holy and wise. He also became a brilliant storyteller. He told stories about Jesus and people came from far and wide to listen. The people of Wales took St David to their hearts and he became the most powerful man in the land, just as the angel had prophesied.
St David died on the first day of March and on that date he is remembered all across Wales.
● Tell the story of St David and encourage the children to tell of heroes and specially remembered people from their own backgrounds.

● **St Patrick's Day:** Little is known about the boyhood of St Patrick, although it is almost certain that he was born in France. When he was a young man he was shipped to Ireland as a prisoner. After a time he returned to France, but soon felt the call to go back to Ireland to tell the people about Jesus. Patrick travelled for many weeks to the home of the king of Ireland. He arrived just before Easter. In the palace courtyard Patrick built a huge bonfire. The king said that on no account was the fire to be lit, but Patrick ignored the king's orders. He thought that by lighting the fire he would show the people that he had come to Ireland to preach the word of God and that his message would spread like wildfire and never go out. Patrick built a monastery and, after many years, became Bishop of Ireland. On St Patrick's Day, the people of Ireland wear the shamrock to show that they will never forget their patron saint.

● Show the children what the shamrock looks like. Talk about four-leafed clover, about the good luck it is supposed to bring. Make a green display surrounded by shamrock or clover shapes cut from green paper.

● **Easter:** (Easter Sunday falls between 22nd March and 25th April, depending on the moon.) Tell the Easter story. Tell the sequence of events during Holy Week from the triumphal entry of Jesus to Jerusalem riding on a donkey, through to the Last Supper and on to the sad and solemn events of Good Friday. Tell the story of the empty grave and how Jesus rose again.

● Perhaps it is a good idea to end the Easter story with the happy meeting of the risen Christ with Mary in the garden and of his walking with Peter by the shore.

● Buy or make hot cross buns. Serve them buttered as part of the Easter assembly. Ask the children if they can guess why they are topped with a cross.

● **Easter eggs:** In most countries and many religions, eggs are seen as a symbol of new life and a new beginning. Talk about new beginnings and signs of spring. Tell about some of the various customs to do with eggs from around the world: egg-rolling, dyeing and decorating eggs, giving chocolate eggs. In some countries there is a kind of egg hide-and-seek; in others, eggs are coloured red or green and exchanged with friends.

GROUP ACTIVITIES

● **Easter eggs:** See photograph and instructions on previous page.

● Organise an egg-rolling contest and give prizes for the most colourful designs.

● **March winds:** Read 'Windy Playground'. Go out and feel the wind blowing through your hair, letting *'the wind bully you'*. What do you think the poet means? Find other words which describe how the wind feels. Make soapy bubbles and watch them float on the wind. Find movement words for bubbles.

● Think of toys which depend on the wind to make them move: kites, windmills, balloons. Find or draw pictures of machines which depend on the power of the wind.

● Can you experiment with bits and pieces from the junk box to make toys which need the wind to move them along? You might be able to make a kite or a land yacht.

● Make a windmill for a younger brother or sister. You need a square of stiff card, a pin, a bead, a stick and scissors.

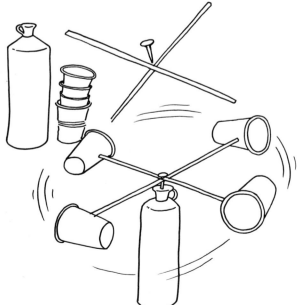

● Make an anemometer (wind-gauge) by using plastic cups and house plant stakes. Hold the gauge outside in the wind and count how many times the cups go round in 30 seconds. (Mark one of the cups to help you count.) Use the wind-gauge each day for a week and find out on which day the wind was strongest.

● **Dolls' Festival:** On 3rd March the Japanese hold a Dolls' Festival or *Hina-Matsuri*. The girls in Japan have special sets of dolls which are brought out on this day. Celebrate by asking the children to bring in dolls from other lands and make a display with books and pictures.

- **Here be Dragons:** Use the salt dough recipe (on page 72) to make a dragon family; or make dragons from the junk box. Set them against a fiery background of tissue paper flames in red, yellow and orange. Find stories, poems and legends about dragons and make a 'dragon-friendly' area.

- Talk about the dragon's fiery breath. When would dragon fire come in handy? For making toast? Lighting birthday candles? Encourage the children to be imaginative in their answers and suggest a drama activity as a follow-up.

- In groups, find good and bad images of fire. Make a large illustrated group book showing that we need fire for warmth, cooking, making pots, etc. and how bad it can be when it is out of control: bush fires, forest fires, house fires. Talk about fire fighters and perhaps arrange a visit to the local fire station.

- Make posters illustrating the message *Never play with fire!* and ask the fire fighters to choose the most effective poster.

WRITING ACTIVITIES

- **If I were an artist:** Read 'Portrait of a Dragon' and make up a 'copycat' poem. Design the most colourful, most incredible dragon anyone could ever imagine. You can borrow anything from the depths of the earth to outer space. Imagine - you can make your dragon's head from the moon and paint it to match the stars!
- Before you begin your poem, list the essential parts of the dragon's body: head, back, spikes, wings, tail - with eyes, teeth and, of course, fire. Then let your imagination run riot!

> *If I were an artist*
> *I'd paint the portrait of a dragon.*
> *For his head I'd borrow the sun.*
> *I'd paint it the colour of poppies*
> *growing in a field of corn.*

- **March winds:** With infant children make simple wind images.
  > *The wind is like a horse galloping.*
  > *The wind is like a fish swimming.*

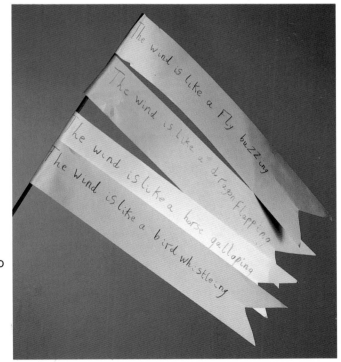

Write each image out on A4 paper, cut into lengthway strips. Add a little picture and cut a V-shape in the end.

- Tape four wind image strips on to an old ruler or a house plant stick. Go outside and run in the wind with your very own wind poem.

- Read 'Windy Playground' and think about what the wind can do to our clothes, to buildings, to fences, to ships at sea. Find a set of movement words, e.g. bend, break, toss, puff, blast. Now use some of these words and ideas to make a set of wind kennings, like this:
  > *The wind is*
  > *A branch-bender*   *wave-tosser*
  > *a coat-teaser*   *a cloud-puffer*

● **Blow wind blow:** With infant children, draw or paint a washing line, collage-style. Make up a rhythmic repetitive poem about the washing dancing in the wind, adding one item each time.

Blow wind blow

Make Dad's shirt dance
with my red skirt,
my red skirt, my red skirt.
Blow wind blow!

Make Dad's shirt dance
with my red skirt,
and Tom's blue shorts,
Tom's blue shorts, Tom's blue shorts.
Blow wind blow!

The children can perform this poem, each holding up their painting in turn.

● **The Invisible Child:** Imagine being invisible, like the wind (see Talking Together). Write a story about being an invisible child. Imagine listening in to kidnappers plotting, to bank robbers planning a raid, to international spies discussing tactics. Imagine giving this information to the police, going along with them on their quest to foil the plotters - after all, they might be glad of an invisible child's help! Make it a very exciting adventure story.

● **It's spring!** Read John Foster's poem 'It's Spring'. He talks about the garden changing its clothes for spring. Write a copycat poem describing what the park, the school field, the woods will wear for spring.

● In March we see the first daffodils of the year. There are a few catkins and primroses and lots of buds beginning to unwind on the trees. March is a yellow and green month. Instead of painting a picture about March colours, you can write a colour poem. Think about what kind of colour yellow is, and put each idea into two lines. Your yellow poem might look like this:

Yellow is the sunshine
dancing in the sky.
Yellow is a primrose
hiding in the grass.

Now write a poem about green, using the same pattern.

ART ACTIVITIES
● **Mother's Day:** Design a special bookmark for Mother's Day. Give it an all-over pattern with *I love my mum* printed in different colours of felt-tip pens, so that the message overlaps. Then fit the bookmark inside a corner card. You could put a few dried flowers or a folded poem in the card as well.

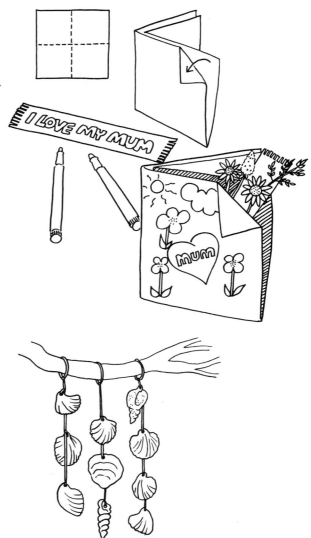

● Find other ways of making Mother's Day cards, as zig-zags, as flap cards, as a card in a pocket, as a shadowed cut-out. Write a poem for your mother and hide it in the card.

● **Wind chime:** Make a wind chime using seashells. This requires the help of an adult using an electric drill to make a hole in the top of each shell. Tie the shells at inervals on lengths of coloured string and hang from the lower branches of a tree. They will chime in the wind as they move.

- **March wind mobiles:** Make a mobile using basic instructions on page 10. Draw two child figures and brightly-coloured kites, again on thin card, cut out and glue in position on the frame. Use tissue paper or scraps of baby ribbon knotted on string. Tape the strings in place to make the kites 'fly'.

- **Mad March Sun:** Read Gina Douthwaite's 'Mad March Sun'. Make a collage frieze with one side in the sunshine, buds and green shoots showing, the other a wintry picture with bare trees and a grey sky.

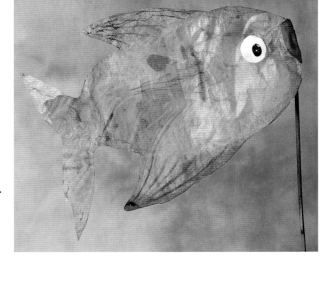

- **Fish kites:** Make kites shaped like fish. Dip single sheets of coloured tissue paper into a marbling solution. Leave to dry, paint-side up. When the paper is dry, put two sheets back to back and draw, then cut out, a fish shape through both sheets. Use a pipe cleaner to reinforce the open mouth and glue into position. When the kite is thoroughly dry, thread a string through either side of the mouth and tie on to a house plant stick. Run in the wind with your fish kite and watch it fly.

- Make Easter cards in the shape of an egg decorated with patterns in wax resist.

April

The Sun's Game
The clouds and the sun
were having a game.
First it was sunshine,
then shadows came.

Spreading and closing,
yellow then blue,
flowers in their pots
didn't know what to do!
Irene Rawnsley

Hatching Eggs
Daniel wrote 'D' on his egg
and Carly pencilled a 'C'.
Trish drew a face on hers
but Martin just wrote 'Me'.

One was left for Emma,
absent with chicken pox.
We placed it with the others
in the incubator box.

'How long will it take,' we asked,
'Before our chicks are born?'
'Twenty-one days,' our teacher said,
'as long as we keep them warm.'

We listened every day until
the chicks began to squeak,
a pattern of cracks appeared
then someone saw a beak!

Our eyes were window wide
as the little chicks broke free.
It wasn't every day we saw
such magic in Class 1B.
Brian Moses

Flamenco
Days dance into summer
wearing new green shoes
and yellow skirts, toes
tapping to tambourines
shaken in the treetops.
Moira Andrew

Rainbows
A rainbow is a painted smile
turned upside down.
It's a multi-coloured bridge
spanning the streets of town.

A rainbow is a brilliant band
across my sister's hair.
It's a steep-sided mountain
piercing the morning air.

A rainbow is a skipping rope
for our playground game.
It's a splash of coloured ink
lighting the sky with flame.

A rainbow is a promise
made before time grew old.
It's a mysterious magic place
hiding a pot of gold.
Moira Andrew

Rain
Rain runs
like beads
from a broken string
like eels
with the river dry
like mice when
blades attack the wheat
like mercury

like ants
from a lifted stone
like links
of a chain
like hours lost
in a sandy glass
like time
runs rain
Irene Rawnsley

TALKING TOGETHER
- **St George's Day:** 23rd April is the feast day of St George, patron saint of England. This celebration tends to be more muted than those of the patron saints of Wales, Scotland and Ireland.
- Look at a map of Great Britain and talk about the lands that go to make it up. Look at the size of England compared to the rest of Britain. Talk about the great towns, rivers and mountains of England. Learn to point them out on the map.

● **April mobile:** Use basic instructions for mobile, on page 10, adding green leaves and a nest with eggs.

● Talk about the different regions of England and listen to tapes of varying accents. Collect postcards of holiday places, famous churches, places of interest, and put them together in a scrap book of England, with emphasis on differences - towns/villages, built-up areas/wide open spaces, seaside/countryside.

● Look at the flag of St. George and its place in the Union Jack. Look for the emblems of the other nations within the Union flag.

● **Shakespeare's birthday** (23rd April): Tell the stories of some of Shakespeare's plays. Ask children to find out as much as they can about the life and work of Shakespeare. Bring in sets of the plays, from tiny pocket books to bound tomes, and make a table display. Add pictures of the Globe Theatre, Anne Hathaway's cottage, Stratford. Make it into a Shakespeare resource centre.

● It might be possible to take the children to a version of one of Shakespeare's plays specially produced for children. Talk to members of the cast afterwards.

● Write and illustrate a book about the visit.

● **Signs of spring:** Look for birds carrying nest materials, for frog spawn, for spring flowers appearing in the gardens and in the hedgerows. Draw the signs of spring and make notes (dated) in your nature notebooks.

● Read 'Hatching Eggs' by Brian Moses. Hire an incubator and try hatching duck or hen eggs. Watch their progress and note each change, until the magic day when the chicks hatch out. Make a calendar of hatching, marked Day 1, Day 2, and so on.

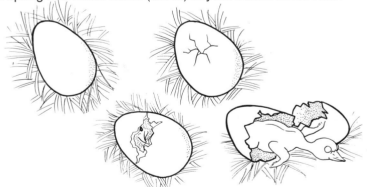

● **April showers:** Read Irene Rawnsley's 'The Sun's Game' in which she says *'flowers in their pots/didn't know what to do!'* April is reputed to be the month of showers, of sun and rain. Note each day's weather carefully in your weather diaries, (see January) to check if April is all it is made out to be!

ASSEMBLIES
● **Easter:** See March.
● **Mothering Sunday:** Mothering Sunday is celebrated on the fourth Sunday of Lent, so will fall in either March or April. Tell about young people who worked away from home, often as domestic servants. They usually sent a portion of their wages home to help the family finances. On Mothering Sunday the girls had a day off to visit their mothers, and took presents of flowers and cakes.

- Bake Mothering Day buns - yeast buns decorated with 'hundreds and thousands', and let the children take them to their mothers with a Mother's Day card (see March).

- **Family festivals:** Like Mothering Sunday in Britain, many other cultures celebrate family festivals in the spring. Spring means renewal, and as such, it is often seen as a time to renew ties with the family.
- The Chinese celebrate spring with the festival of *Ch'ing Ming,* a happy family occasion of new clothes, good food and catching up on news.
- The Muslims' spring festival is *Eid ul-Fitr* when families visit and exchange presents.

- **St George's Day:** On St George's Day, tell the saint's story as far as it is known. St George was a soldier who is thought to have fought with the Crusaders as tales of his bravery were brought back by men returning from the Crusades. Despite cruelty and torture, St George remained true to his Christian faith and was put to death by unbelievers, possibly in Palestine.
- Tell the legend that has grown up about St George and his fight with the dragon.
- Tell stories of English heroes and heroines, e.g. Grace Darling, Captain Scott, Florence Nightingale. Talk about the difference between true stories and legends.

GROUP ACTIVITIES
- **Mothers and babies:** This is the best time of the year to visit a farm. Look out for lambs, calves and chicks. This is an ideal opportunity to teach the children the basics of photography. Put together an album of photographs recording the visit.
- With the younger children, make a scrap book of pictures and drawings, emphasising mother and baby animals.
- With older children, use the farm visit as a starting point for work on life cycles.
- Make up charts using diagrams, photographs and drawings showing one child's progression from babyhood to school age. Make a display of socks and shoes to demonstrate how children's feet have grown since they were born. Show their growth on bar charts and graphs.

- **Wild flowers:** By the beginning of April, many wild flowers will have put in an appearance, depending on where you live. With the warmer weather it is often possible to take the children out on a nature walk.
- Make identification of wild flowers into a competition, always insisting that children 'take the book to the flower', so that flowers are left undisturbed. Encourage children to make rough sketches of those they have found, noting shape, colour and habitat. Later, the drawings can be transferred, in greater detail, to their nature notebooks. (See Art Activities.)
- Read 'Flamenco', and think about what you have found in the hedgerows and fields that might fit in with the idea of *new green shoes/and yellow skirts.* Make a list of all the yellow flowers you can find that bloom in April. If it is not possible to go on a nature walk, look in books about wild flowers and hedgerows.

- **All Fools' Day:** 1st April is a day to watch out for in schools! Suggest that children use that day to demonstrate any magic tricks with disappearing coins or moving glasses that they know, and organise a Magic Show in the classroom.
- There is an old country saying about 1st April,
  If it thunders on All Fools' Day
  It brings good crops of corn and hay.
  Do you think this is true? Can you find any more sayings about April? If you do, add them to your nature notebook and try to find out later in the year if any of them come true.
- Find out about jesters and clowns. Why do you think clowns paint their faces? Make a collage of clown faces and think of jokes that they could tell. (See Art Activities.) Make up a joke book in each group.

- **Rainbows:** April is the month of sun and showers, just the weather for rainbows. Watch to see how many you have seen this month. Look for stories and poems about rainbows and find out the sequence of colours. Make a zig-zag book and colour each page with pencil crayons, following the colours of the rainbow. Put cut-out pictures of red things on the red page, purple things on the purple page, and so on.
- Look at the colours in a prism when the sun shines through it. Think of other places where you can find the colours of a rainbow.

- Bring in and look at kaleidoscopes, where you can see colours and patterns reflected like rainbows in mirrors.
- You can make a kaleidoscope from stiff card, foil, clear plastic and some coloured beads.

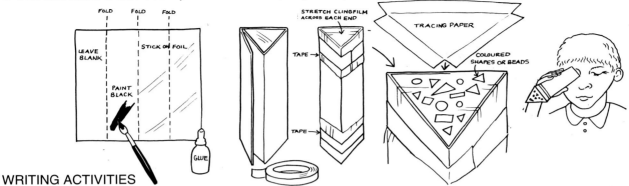

WRITING ACTIVITIES

- **The Shakespeare Hats:** To celebrate Shakespeare's birthday, make a collection of 'story' hats: police hats, firefighters' hats, hard hats, wedding hats, caps, shawls etc. Imagine that you can become William Shakespeare for the day, able to invent your own characters, all suggested by wearing different hats.
- Each child wearing a hat takes on a new identity. Let them tell the story of the person wearing the hat, or make up a poem from the hat-wearer's point of view. It might even be a magic hat!
- Ask children to make up a dialogue, each 'masked' by wearing someone else's hat. Make it funny or sad or combative. Perhaps a group could later make a short scripted piece from the original spontaneous dialogue.

- **Rainbows:** Use the rainbow as the basis for an image poem. This can be a simple oral exercise with the youngest children. Look at a picture of a rainbow and ask what it looks like: bridge, slide, happy face, hairband, etc. An oral response of this kind is a first step to work on simile and metaphor - the bedrock of poetry.

- Read 'Rainbows' by Moira Andrew and make up a copycat poem, using your own set of images.

    A rainbow is like an umbrella
        opened out against the rain.
    It is like a stripey mushroom
        growing in the dark grey sky.

In the example shown in the photograph, Aurelia has turned her image poem on the rainbow into a riddle.

- **April Fool's Day:** Work with a partner and collect all the silliest April Fool jokes you can think of. Put them together to make a list poem. This poem works best if it rhymes, especially if the rhymes are so silly that they are really funny!

- **Recipe for spring:** Use a recipe format to put together a poem to celebrate spring. Gather together the 'ingredients', so your poem begins:

    Take the green of waking leaves,
    the yellow of morning sunshine
    and the pale pink of cherry blossom.

To finish the poem continue with the recipe format, **_Add_** (3 lines), **_Mix in_** (3 lines), **_Decorate with_** (3 lines). (See Recipe for Winter, page 39.)

- **St George and the Dragon:** Tell the story of St George and the dragon as if you were one of the by-standers. Make it into a newspaper report for the local paper. Find a really catchy headline, one which will stand out on the newsvendor's board and make people want to buy the paper.

- **Pot of Gold:** Think of the story about a pot of gold at the end of the rainbow. Imagine that you are going in search of the treasure. This is a really difficult task and you meet trolls and dragons, wise women and kings, robbers and pirates, before you reach your goal.
- Make your story into an up-to-date legend, perhaps with spaceships and aircraft to get you from one place to another. Plan your story, adventure by adventure, in note form before you get down to the serious business of writing. This can be a project which takes several days to complete.
- For infants, use a zig-zag book with shaped contours on the top of each page to suggest an environment in which each part of the Pot of Gold story takes place, e.g. a turreted shape to suggest a castle, a pointed shape to suggest a mountain, etc.

- Both the Pot of Gold story and St George and the Dragon can be told in comic strip format. This is a more difficult writing task than it first appears, as the children have to make decisions about the main characters through whom the story is told. Then they have to keep the momentum of the story going with just a few words of dialogue or a brief summary under each picture sequence.

- **Rain:** Read 'Rain' by Irene Rawnsley. It is made up of a series of images: rain like beads, like eels, like ants etc. Use the 'shopping list' method to start children off on images of their own. Encourage them to imagine where these images are, e.g. *'like ants/from a lifted stone'*. Use some of the children's ideas to write a class copycat poem about rain, and follow this by encouraging the children to make up their own image poems.

- **Dance of spring:** Read 'Flamenco' by Moira Andrew and talk about different kinds of dancing. Look for pictures of what clothes a dancer might wear in ice dancing, ballet, tap-dancing etc. and write a poem about spring with a different dance in mind. Ask everyone to use the same first line, then extend it, thinking of spring colours linked to each kind of dance. It might look like this:

    Days dance into summer
    wearing pink ballet shoes
    and cherry blossom skirts,
    toes pointing to primroses
    hiding in the hedgerows.
- Listen to the sounds of the rain and make up a sound poem using words like *splash, sprinkle, gush, flow.*

- **Who lives in the tree?:** With the youngest infants, make up a poem from a list of animals and birds who might make their homes in a tree. Use the adjective, noun, verb pattern:

    a wise owl hooting
    a furry squirrel leaping
    a black bat sleeping
Write out the poem inside a tree shape which opens to reveal words and pictures (see photograph, page 53).

ART ACTIVITIES
- **The Shakespeare Hats:** Using crêpe paper, scraps of material, feathers, ribbons, etc. make fantastic hats and masks to use as 'story hats'. (See Writing Activities.) Have a competition to see who can design a hat offering the most scope for an unusual character for modern William Shakespeares to write about.

Who is hiding in the tree?

Is it...
a barn owl hooting?
a red squirrel leaping?
a baby bird hatching?
a bright Woodpecker pecking?

Look and see!

See Writing Activity 'Who lives in the tree?' on facing page

● **Wild flowers:** On your nature walks make pencil sketches of different wild flowers, trying in particular to show shape and form. Back in the classroom, experiment with different media: pencil crayon, oil-based pastels, poster paints. Have a wild flower display with each flower neatly labelled and invite parents to the show. Afterwards, add the drawings to your nature notebooks.

● **Clowns and Jesters:** Find pictures of clowns with painted faces. Use these as patterns to make a clown collage. Use A4 size (or larger) and fill the page with a face shape. Paint sad faces, happy faces, excited faces, exaggerating the emotions and using bright primary colours. Make a crowded clown collage and write out your best jokes to make a border. (See Group Activities.)
● Make a jester collage in the same way.

● **The Sun's Game:** Read Irene Rawnsley's poem, 'The Sun's Game'. Make a 'sunshine and showers' class picture with one side showing clouds, shadows and raindrops; the other, sunshine and bright wide-open flowers. Put a title 'The flowers didn't know what to do!'

● **Rainbow T-shirts:** If there is good weather and you can venture outside for an afternoon, use the idea of rainbow colours as the basis for a tie-dye session. Use white T-shirts and mix a range of rainbow coloured dyes in separate containers. Roll up the T-shirt and tie it tightly at intervals with string. Knot the string tightly. Choose one of the colours and submerge the tied-up T-shirt in the dye for a few minutes. (Make sure that the children wear rubber gloves.) Wait until it is almost dry and undo the ties. Then let the T-shirt dry out. When it is quite dry, go through the whole process again, tying in a different place and using another colour of dye. Hang to dry.
● Let the children model their rainbow T-shirts for an assembly when the story of Noah's Ark is told. Then arrange for the young poets to read some of their rainbow image poems.

● **Lilliput jungle:** Dig up a sod of grass and let the children draw what they can see, but enlarging and exaggerating each blade of grass. Now ask them to make it into a jungle environment, adding butterflies, lizards, snakes and animals drawn in bright oil-based pastels, cut out and pasted into the relatively tall grasses.

May

May Day
Oak and ivy, sycamore, ash,
Hawthorn, ivy, sycamore, oak.
Wash your face in the May dew,
Wish, then take your chance;
Jack-in-the-Green or Maypole Queen,
Who'll join in the Maypole dance?
Hawthorn, sycamore, ivy, oak,
Oak and ivy, sycamore, ash.
                    (part poem) *Judith Nicholls*

May Poem
rain falls

the candy-floss tree
rains confetti and
bridesmaids

Pink snowdrifts
lie on the path
                    Gerda Mayer
('May Poem' from *Expression No. 7, 1967*)

Grass Music
Wind sways the grasses on the hill
their names dance in my head:
Timothy and Cocksfoot,
Ryegrass and Brome
everywhere I tread.

Wind sways the grasses on the hill
their names sing strange and sweet:
Meadow Foxtail,
Quaking grass,
Yorkshire Fog at my feet.
                    Sheila Simmons

Spring in the City
Cherry trees
stand guard
on pavements,
unclench
their fists,
hold out
handfuls of
blossom
to explode
like party poppers
in the sun.
                    Moira Andrew

Images of May
Bluebells blur
the grass like
    smoke from
a tinker's fire.

Beech leaves
thread pale lace
    through the
last of the sun.

Underfoot, ferns
uncoil question
    marks in
answer to spring.
                    Moira Andrew

TALKING TOGETHER
- **May Day:** Read 'May Day' by Judith Nicholls. The poem tells how country people used to walk in procession waving branches and blossom to celebrate the first day of May - and the coming of summer. How many different trees does Judith Nicholls mention? Try to find them in your tree book. (See Group Activities.)
- May Day festivals stem from Roman times when Flora, the Goddess of Flowers, was honoured. The May Queen, crowned with flowers, represents Flora herself and the Maypole symbolises fertility. Talk about folk festivals, Morris dancers and different ways of welcoming summer. Find out if there are unusual local customs connected with May Day.
- Morris dancers are often accompanied by a Fool or a Hobby-horse. 'Oss, the famous Cornish Hobby-horse, is brought out to help celebrate May Day in Padstow. He wears a mask and a hat and chases young girls along the street. When he catches one, it is supposed to bring her luck. Find pictures of 'Oss and make a wall frieze, showing the harbour, houses, by-standers, Morris dancers and, of course, 'Oss himself.

Maypole Dance, see page 59

- Beltane is a Celtic festival still sometimes celebrated in Scotland by lighting great bonfires on the hilltops at the end of the day. Talk about other times when bonfires are important.
- In Oxford, May Day is celebrated by the choristers of Magdalen College who climb the tower and sing a hymn in Latin to welcome the sunrise. This is followed by a peal of bells and dancing in the streets.

- **May proverb:** *Mist in May, heat in June,*
  Makes the harvest come right soon.
  This is an old country prediction about the weather. Can you think of any other sayings or proverbs about May? Note as many as you can find in your nature notebook. If you record each day's weather you can check if there is any truth in them.
- **May blossom:** Read 'May Poem' by Gerda Mayer. Talk about the *'candy-floss tree'*. What does the poet mean? Do you pass trees looking like this on your way to school? How many different trees in blossom can you find?
- **Here we come gathering nuts in May:** Sing the old rhyme with the children. Of course, there are no nuts in May, but it is thought that the nuts refer to 'knots' of May blossom which were among the branches gathered by the people who danced round the village.
- There is a tradition that the first person to find a branch of hawthorn in full bloom got a dish of cream as a reward. Another says that if young girls go out at dawn on May Day and wash their faces in hawthorn dew it will make them very beautiful.
- Talk about some of the old May Day traditions. Use them to make new words to fit the old rhyme.
  Here we come washing our faces in dew
  or   *Here we come waving our branches in May*
  or   *Here we come dancing around the Maypole*
  Invent as many verses as you can, and dance to a percussion or piano accompaniment.

- **Bird survey:** Nesting activity is at its height during the month of May. Set up a nest box in the playground, well away from stray cats, but as close to the classroom window as possible. Watch to see if birds are attracted to the box, but don't go too near.
- Talk about the best way to set up a bird survey: a tick sheet, graph, notes and pictures? Each group might choose a different method. Use bird books to check identity of each new species visiting the bird tray or school grounds.
- As a class you might wish to join the RSPB or Young Ornithologists' Club. Both have some excellent literature and suggest interesting projects.

ASSEMBLIES

- **The Glastonbury Thorn:** Tell the story of the famous Glastonbury Thorn which is said to have sprung from the staff of Joseph of Arimathea who came with his followers to bring Christianity to the Britons. On Christmas Day, so the story goes, when Joseph was preaching to the people, he banged his staff on the ground to emphasise a point and it immediately became a young hawthorn tree covered in white blossom. The people were so amazed that they built a church there to thank God for the message that Joseph had brought. You can still see a thorn tree at Glastonbury and it is reputed to blossom every year at Christmas time.
- If you are close enough to visit, a trip to Glastonbury Abbey is very worthwhile.

- Look out for hawthorn trees and hedges. Cut a branch and bring it into school. Look at the delicate blossom and gently feel the cruel thorns. It is thought that Christ's crown of thorns might have been fashioned from branches of the hawthorn.

- **Flower festivals:** May is the month when the hedgerows begin to bloom and the gardens start to show summer colour. Many churches hold flower festivals towards the end of May.

- Hold a flower festival in school and invite parents to join children and teachers in a service of thanks for the coming of summer. Afterwards, make the flowers into attractive bouquets and take them (tagged with cards made by the children) to sick or housebound members of the local community.

- Many other countries and cultures hold flower festivals. The Japanese hold a Hollyhock Festival on l5th May when hollyhocks are brought to the temples. In ancient days the Chinese too held a flower festival in the month of May when women and children wore paper flowers which they had made themselves.

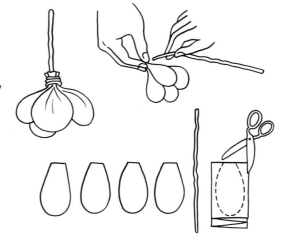

- Try making flowers with crêpe and tissue paper for a special flower ceremony. Everyone, including the teachers, can wear flowers which they have made. It makes a very colourful and different assembly to welcome summer.

- **Well Dressing:** In some English villages May brings the old custom of well-dressing. After the Black Death, where wells had not become contaminated, the local people gathered to give thanks for pure water. They made posies of flowers and threw them into the water. Now they make garlands and pictures with flowers and place them round the top of the well.
- Take a glass of water into assembly and talk about it as a precious gift for which we should give thanks. Talk about those countries where war and drought means that water is scarce, where the people have to walk many dusty miles to the nearest well to bring back enough water for just one day.
- Work out how many litres of water an average family is likely to use in a day in our country. It might be possible to link this service with a collection to go towards the provision of a water pipe for Somalia, or some other country where drought kills.

- **Blessing the Sea:** This ceremony is still held in some fishing villages around Ascension Day (the fortieth day after Easter). It is a festival to bless the fruits of the earth and to ask God's blessing on the coming fishing season. Church officials and congregations go in procession to the harbour and often a service is conducted in the RNLI lifeboat station.
- If appropriate, it might be an opportunity to ask members of the RNLI to school to talk to the children about the work they do.

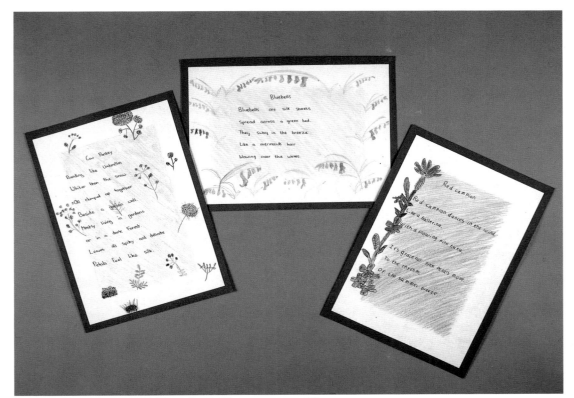

See Mini-poems, in Writing Activities on page 58

GROUP ACTIVITIES

● **Maypole Dance:** In some schools the old tradition of dancing round the Maypole is followed. Failing a Maypole, there are a number of very effective folk dances, such as the Ribbon Dance, which are worth learning, and have a flavour of the ancient May Day festivities. (See photograph on page 55.)

● **Trees:** Read 'May Poem' and 'Spring in the city'. Look at trees in blossom. Draw and label your drawings to add to your nature notebooks.

● **Grass Music:** Look at a book about grasses (e.g. the Pan book of *Grasses, Ferns and Lichens* by Roger Phillips) and see if it is possible to identify different grasses on a nature walk. Pick a few stems, press and label them. We tend to think of grass just as grass, but there is a huge variety, as Sheila Simmons points out in her poem.

● If there is a breeze, lie with your ear to the ground and listen to the sound of the grass swaying. Can you make up grass music? Try it out with bells and shakers when you get back to school. Set Sheila Simmons' poem to music.

● **Branch Weaving:** If you are out and about early you will see spiders' webs on the grass. Look at the delicacy of their weaving. You can make webs on a grand scale using branches.
Each group needs a large dead branch, some strips of cloth (of varying widths), wool or ribbons. You will also need a ball of string. Tie the string around the branch, knotting it between the smaller branches and the main upright to make a kind of random web. Then weave the strips of cloth and ribbons over and under the string. Use shades of one colour to give the best effect and add glass beads or buttons to look like drops of dew. Hang the finished branch weaving from the ceiling across the corner of the hall or classroom.

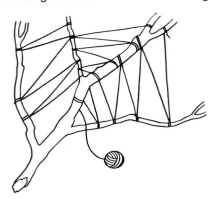
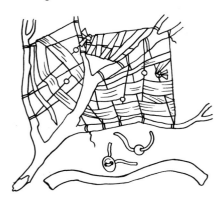

- **Hedgerows:** Look at the hedges in May and you will be surprised by how many white flowers there are. Identify as many white flowers as you can find. Draw, label, date and add to your nature notebook.
- White cow parsley, bluebells, Red Campion are all flowers which bloom in May. Can you find others? Put the wild flowers of May into colour sets. (See Mini-poems, in Writing Activities.)

WRITING ACTIVITIES
- **Images of May:** Read 'Images of May'. The poet has thought of three pictures which are special to this month - bluebells, beech leaves, ferns uncurling. Close your eyes and think of three pictures, like photographs in colour, which mean May to you. Now put each idea into four short lines, to make a copycat poem.
- The poet says *'bluebells blur/the grass like/smoke'*. Have you ever seen crowds of bluebells spilling across the grass? Make a picture in your mind's eye and find other ways of describing them - like a wave splashing? like a blue blanket spreading?
- **Mini-poems:** Use your descriptions to make a word-picture of bluebells. Try the same idea for cow parsley, May blossom, Red Campion. Write out your mini-poem on a card gently coloured with pencil crayon and edged with flowers. (See photograph on page 57.)

- **Hedgerow music:** Read 'Grass Music'. Look at the way Sheila Simmons has used the names of various grasses to give the poem its rhythm. Say some of the words over in your head,
    Timothy and Cocksfoot,
    Ryegrass and Brome.......
    Meadow Foxtail,
    Quaking grass.......

- Look at your wild flower book and find names of some of the flowers that bloom in May.
  Look for names that sing!
    Spotted Medick, Pheasant's Eye, Dove's Foot Cranesbill, Shepherd's Purse....
  'Top and tail' the flower names as the poet has done to make a music poem of the hedgerow, like this perhaps:
    Breeze blows the hedgerow flowers,
    their names dance in my head:
    Spotted Medick, Pheasant's Eye
    everywhere I tread.

Or, better still, make up your own 'top and tail' for the poem.

- **The Glastonbury Thorn:** Write a diary as though you were one of Joseph of Arimathea's followers. Tell how you boarded a boat in a land of sunshine, navigated stormy waters until you landed in a cold unfamiliar country, where people spoke an unintelligible language. (Find out how long such a voyage would have taken.) Tell how you made friends, found shelter, listened to Joseph telling the people about Jesus.
- Imagine that you were a by-stander on the day when the Glastonbury Thorn miraculously appeared. Write down every detail so that you can tell the story to your grandchildren.
- Make up an illustrated brochure to encourage tourists to visit the Glastonbury Thorn. Make it full of interest and excitement, suggesting the best time of year to visit.

- **Letter from the City:** Write a letter to a penfriend in a country very different from our own. Draw a rough plan of your route to school and describe some of the things you pass. Tell what you can hear and see and how you feel on a sunny morning in May.
- Read 'Spring in the City'. The poet says she sees cherry trees on the pavements, blossom exploding *'like party poppers/in the sun'*. Try to find other unusual images to describe a tree, a garden, the feel of the wind or something you have seen on the way to school.
- Take one image and use it to make a long thin poem like 'Spring in the City'.

- **May Poem:** Read Gerda Mayer's 'May Poem'. Imagine that you, like the poet, are out in the rain. Expand the poem into a page of prose writing, adding details that the poet has had to leave out.

ART ACTIVITIES

- **May Blossom:** Look at cherry, crab-apple, pear trees in blossom. Look at May blossom on the hawthorn. Gerda Mayer says it is like *candy-floss* or *confetti.* Experiment with different media to find your own best way of showing a tree in blossom - you could use paint, coloured pencils or oil-based pastels.

- Display individually, or cut out each tree to make a frieze collage-style in mixed media of a tree-lined street or an orchard.

- Make a mobile in thin card showing the outline of a tree - using the basic instructions on page 10. Add leaves made from card and use tissue paper (laid flat, not scrunched up) to make blossom.

Grass music: Read Sheila Simmons' poem. Look at the way in which wind makes grasses sway. Use crayons or oil-based pastels to create the effect of wind. Make the grasses a series of lines all drawn in the same direction, almost like falling rain. This gives rhythm to the drawing and gives a feeling of movement.

- **Maypole Dance:** With the youngest children get each one to paint a colourful dancing figure. Cut out and paste collage-style on a Maypole background with each dancer holding a ribbon. (See photograph on page 55.)

- Make a group poem (See 'Nuts in May') and write out each part on Maypole ribbons to make an effective display of written work. You could add cut-out dancers to give it more colour.

- **Well-dressing:** Make group pictures to celebrate the gift of water, using a collage of flowers cut from seed packets or garden catalogues. The pictures can also be created from individual flower paintings, again put together collage-style to make an overall well-dressing picture. Paint a well outline and arrange the flower pictures against it.

June

Racing my Shadow
I know my shadow's with me
In the shade of the oak tree.
I cannot see it anywhere
But it must be watching me.
For every time I make a dash
From shade into the sun
It races out ahead of me,
However fast I run.

John Coldwell

Like Purple Aeroplanes
They used to fly
over all the ponds
in summer, Granny says -

like sparkling sapphire helicopters,
purple aeroplanes,
with eyes of bright topaz,
wings flashing emerald light,
brightening the countryside
in their jewelled flight.

I hope I'll see one someday,
hope they'll come back again,
dragon-fly........whisper it,
magical name.

Joan Poulson

Nature Study
This butterfly
we couldn't identify
   pitched
its bright tent
on a roadside flower.

For a full minute,
outstretched wings
   bloodied
the morning air
in studied symmetry.

Our eyes ached
with raw colour
   remembered
pattern and shape
against eventual flight.

It drifted away
and precise geometry
   lingered
like an after image
in the yellow heat.

Moira Andrew

June Tune
O Wind-In-The-Grasses, bee in the briar -
The Meadow her mother, the Sun her sire;
Weave her a web of flowers and fire.
She has wings
And warmly sings
Of bright colour in a buttercup
til evening shut her up,
In a blossom that a moonbeam swings.

David R. Morgan

TALKING TOGETHER

- **Sundials:** This is the magic month when the sun rides high in the sky and shadows grow long. Read John Coldwell's 'Racing My Shadow'. Talk about sundials and how shadows can help to tell the time. A sundial is a shadow clock which was invented thousands of years ago - the earliest date from 300 BC. With their interest in mathematics, the Greeks developed very complicated sundials. In the 1600s, sundials were gradually overtaken by the invention of clocks.

- **Sun worship:** Many ancient peoples worshipped the sun and held festivals in honour of the sun gods. Aztecs and Incas believed that the sun was the giver of all life. In Europe, people lit bonfires and carried blazing torches through the streets. They thought that the flames would give their power to the sun and so hold back the ebbing days of summer.

- Talk about the ceremonies which are traditionally held at Stonehenge to celebrate the summer solstice. If possible, visit Avebury or Stonehenge. Failing a visit, look at photographs and talk about the history of stone circles.

A green thesaurus (see page 64)

Imagine a world....(see page 64)

● Read stories of Icarus whose wings were made partly of wax. He flew too near the sun and his wings melted, leaving Icarus to plunge into the sea.

● **Hedgerow flowers:** In June the hedgerows blaze with summer colour. Look for wild roses, elderflowers, moon daisies, Herb Robert, speedwell, vetch, Red Campion. Draw and name them in your nature notebooks. (See Writing Activities.)

● Read David Morgan's 'June Tune'. Listen for bees in the flowers and look for butterflies. Name and draw the butterflies. Make butterfly blots with coloured ink.

● **Weather lore:** There is an old saying: *A dripping June, Sets all in tune.*
Can you find any more? Illustrate the weather rhymes and copy them into your nature notebook.

● **Forest Trail:** June is the ideal time to explore a forest or woodland trail. Ask for an information booklet about the forest and talk to the children about what they should look out for or listen to. Look at a plan of the walk, perhaps enlarging it on the classroom wall so that children can add details of special interest. Such pre-planning adds to the excitement and educational value of the visit.

● Use a commercial colour chart for paints. Talk about the names of different greens and browns. Suggest that the children try to invent new names for each green when they visit the forest. This task focuses their attention on the range and variety of one colour - that green alone is like a paintbox! (See Writing Activities.)

● For the youngest children, give each a strip from the colour chart. Suggest that it is a piece of a 'fallen rainbow' which they must match with something they see on the woodland walk.

ASSEMBLIES

● **Trinity Sunday:** The feast day of the Trinity (first Sunday after Whitsun) usually falls in June. It celebrates one of the main Christian tenets, that God is three persons in one, God the Father, Son and Holy Spirit. This is a difficult concept for children to grasp. St Patrick is said to have explained this idea to his followers by showing them a shamrock which although three-lobed, is only one leaf.

- Take three candles and light them. Show that individually each gives a little light, together they give one bright light. Talk about the way three children working together can get things done quickly, how a team of three can pull together and be strong - as in Tug-of-War.
- Tell how Jesus told his disciples to go to people all over the world and *'baptise them in the name of the Father, the Son and the Holy Spirit.'* (Matthew 28: 19).

- **St Barnabas' Day** (11th June): This is said to be the ideal time to begin hay-making:
    On St Barnabas'
    Put the scythe to grass.
  St Barnabas was a Christian missionary (originally called Joseph), a friend and supporter of St Paul, during his early ministry. Later the two friends disagreed and parted company.
  St Barnabas went off alone to Cyprus where he continued to make converts to Christianity.

- **Sunshine Assembly:** It might be possible to take this assembly outside on a sunny morning. Feel the warmth of the sunshine on our bodies. Talk about how we all depend on the sun for light and energy, how it helps trees and flowers to grow.

- Have children dressed as suns, telling about light and shade, about the things the sun can see as it journeys across the skies.

- Make up prayers, giving thanks for the sun.

- **Find sunshine words:** *bright, dazzling, sparkling, glittering.* Make a sunshine display of buckets and spades, swimsuits, sandals, sun umbrellas, sunglasses. (Show sunscreens, stressing why they are necessary.) Make the background in golds, yellows, reds, with sun-words printed across it in sizzling colours.

GROUP ACTIVITIES
- **Shadows:** Read John Coldwell's poem 'Racing My Shadow'. Why do you think the poet can't see his shadow when he is *'in the shade of the oak tree'*? On a sunny day, try an experiment to see if you can outrun your shadow. Where will you need to hide? Try running out into the sunshine and watch how your shadow behaves. Is it racing ahead of you, or following behind?

- **Follow my leader:** Two children can work together for this. Each should have a small mirror to reflect the sun on to a wall. Use the mirrors to chase each other's spot of light across the wall. Don't move your feet, just let the reflections do the 'running'.

● Make shadow clocks which depend on sunlight. You will need a pencil, a cotton reel, Plasticine and a piece of white card. On a bright sunny day put the pencil in to the cotton reel and place it on the white card. Steady it with a piece of Plasticine. Draw a line along the shadow of the stick and mark the time. Set your alarm for one hour later so that you can draw the next shadow and make a note of the time.

● **Forest trail:** On your forest walk, suggest that the youngest children collect as many brown items as they can. Give them a sheet of paper criss-crossed with double-sided adhesive tape and let them stick fallen leaves, bits of twig, cones etc. on to their sheet. (By suggesting brown, it means that the children will not be collecting living plants or leaves.) Try to identify the items in your collection on your return to school.
● Read Joan Poulson's 'Like Purple Aeroplanes'. Watch out for winged insects on the trail, awarding points for identifying particular kinds of butterfly, maximum points for finding a dragonfly! (Use a butterfly book.) This kind of competition encourages children to keep their eyes open to what is going on around them.
● Read 'Nature Study' by Moira Andrew. The poet says that they couldn't identify the butterfly. What colour was it? Can you find one like this in your butterfly book?
● Look for different greens (see Talking Together), using a grid to draw and name each new green, e.g. *prickly green, shadowy green, thorny green* (see Writing Activities).
● Try 'walking on the treetops' using mirrors. Use your mirror to explore an unknown environment by turning it upwards and noting what you can see in the treetops. Work in pairs or as a small group for this task.
● Encourage children to use other senses: listen to the sound of water, of birds, of animals, of cracking twigs, crackling leaves. Put your arms round a tree and listen. Touch the bark with fingertips. Touch the softness of moss, roughness of stones, smoothness of pebbles. If it rains, put out your tongue and taste a raindrop.

● **Wild roses:** Look for wild roses in the hedgerows. Draw the rose in pencil, or pen and ink, trying to keep its delicate character.
● Find out how many institutions use the wild rose as an emblem - rose of England, white rose of York, red rose of Lancaster, Queen Alexandra's Nurses.

WRITING ACTIVITIES
● **Wild flowers:** Look for flowers in the hedgerows and meadows or look in the June section of your Wild Flower book (see Talking Together). Look for interesting-sounding names to use as the chorus for a summer poem.

Sun shines, breeze blows	*Viper's Bugloss, Tufted Vetch,*
Hedges alight with white wild rose,	*Prickly Sowthistle, Queen Anne's Lace.*

● **The Three Bears:** For the youngest children, read or tell the story of the Three Bears. Imagine finding a little house which can't be seen by grown-ups. Who lives there? Bears? Trolls? Aliens? Brainstorm a story with the children. What colour is the house? - not boring old white, but purple-spotted, rainbow-striped!
● Make a zig-zag book for each child, one page for every part of the Three Bears story, or a large group book. Make flaps to hide the porridge bowls, chairs, beds - even Goldilocks! (See Art Activities.)

● **Lost in the Forest:** Work on this poem after a visit, or make the picture of a dense forest your starting point. Collect sets of words on colour, sounds, feelings. Find images to describe trees, branches, roots. Begin by grouping feelings:
Lost, lonely, cold
I am trapped in this deep forest
like a fox in a snare.
Or begin from the sounds of the forest:
Owls hooting, leaves rustling,
wind whistling, animals scurrying,
the only sounds in this deep forest.
This approach allows the writer a direct way into the poem. Discourage the use of *'One day'* or *'Once upon a time'* as this tends to make the poem into a piece of prose. Suggest that the poem finishes when the writer is still trapped alone in the forest, unable to find the way out. (Everyone obviously made it home safely, but that is not part of the poem!) (See Art Activities.)

● **Mini-poems round a tree:** On your visit to the woodland trail ask each child/group to choose a particular tree. Sketch it quickly and begin to make notes for mini image poems to describe different parts of the tree or the animals and birds who make their homes there.

Among the topmost branches: *'Birds sing with joy/ as they play ring-a-roses/among the treetops';* at the base of the tree *'Roots like/writhing snakes/uncoiling.'*

Draw the tree in black fibre-tip pen (or pencil) on white, and write the mini-poems around the picture.

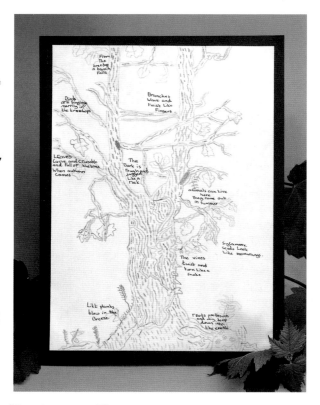

● **A green thesaurus:** Use some of the new green names you have invented (see Talking Together) and put them together as a rhythmic chorus for a green poem. (See photograph on page 61.)
This task invites children to look, to compare, to explore with their eyes, not simply to accept green as the colour of grass.

Green, green, green,
so many greens in the forest,
Misty green, Brambly green,

Ghostly green, Thorny green,
Prickly green, Whispering green,
so many greens in the forest.

● **Imagine a world without trees:** Ask children to think about the things we would miss in a world without trees. Make up a list of ideas. Put them together and display on a doubled sheet of A4 paper. Cut out circular 'spy-holes' marked 'NO!' and draw what we would lose if there were no trees left. (See photograph page 61.)

● **Forest Riddles:** On your forest walk, look out for something which you can describe in an image poem, keeping in mind colour, shape and other details of what you have chosen to write about. Perhaps make your poem into a riddle, and write it in a one-poem book by folding a sheet of paper into four, keeping the fold at the top. Design a cover, write the poem inside, and hide your answer beneath a flap. (See photograph.)

ART ACTIVITIES

- **Lost in the forest:** When the children have written their poem in draft (see Writing Activities), encourage them to look at the shape it will make on the finished page. Write it out on a sheet of green paper or thin A4 card. Leave plenty of room top, bottom and around the sides. Now place another sheet on top of the poem and outline the shape of the poem in pencil. (Use a sunny window.) Make a forest frame for the poem, filling it in with felt-tip pens or coloured pencils. Then cut out the hole and paste your frame around the poem. (See photograph.)

- Framing other poems in this way is also very effective, especially when the content suggests an uneven or wavy outline.

- **The Three Bears:** Using salt dough (see recipe on page 72), make a plaque of the three bears. After baking, paint with poster paints and varnish in the usual way when the paint has dried. Each group could make a plaque of a different stage in the story: the deep forest, Goldilocks running away, bowls of porridge on the table, etc.

- **Pressed flowers:** Gather a few fresh flowers - use buttercups, daisies or dandelions (not rare specimens). Lay the flowers out on an old newspaper so that they don't touch. Put another sheet of paper on top. Put heavy books on top of the newspaper and leave the flowers to dry. (This takes about four weeks.) Arrange the pressed flowers on a bookmark or on the front of a home-made card. Glue lightly into place.

- **Shadow patterns:** Read John Coldwell's poem 'Racing My Shadow'. On a sunny day look at shadow shapes in the playground and make a rough drawing of a variety of interesting shapes: a child standing alone, a tree, the school building, the gate. Back inside the classroom, make shadow patterns in black on a colour. They will look quite abstract, unconnected with their starting points.
- Each child should paint a moving figure: running, skipping, hopping. When the paint is dry, cut out. Now turn the cut-out over, and use the shape as a template to make a shadow in black. Glue on a background frieze to make a picture of a busy playground on a sunny day.

- **Dragonflies:** Read Joan Poulson's 'Like Purple Aeroplanes'. Use a reference book to find out about dragonflies. Paint a summer pond with goldfish, bullrushes and waterlilies. Add hovering dragonflies made from bright tissue paper glued flat.

July

Spot-a, Spot-a Sports Day

Chuck-a, chuck-a discus,
put-a, put-a shot,
jet-a, jet-a javelin,
lap-a, lap-a lot.

Pick-a, pick-a partner -
link-a, link-a leg.
Run-a, run-a relay,
splodge-a, splodge a' egg.

Trick-a, trick-a teacher -
slit-a, slit-a sack.
Puff-a, puff-a parent
round, around a track.

Spot-a, spot-a sports day,
what a lot o'rain!
Not a spot o' sunshine.
Call it off, again.

Gina Douthwaite

Count me out

It's not that
I'm a scaredy cat,
it's just that
I don't like caves
and the feeling of doom
in the colourless gloom
flowing over you
in waves.

It's the way
your voice rolls
round and around,
echoing low and weird,
and your torch becomes
such a little light,
each shadow one
to be feared.

It's the way
the clammy cold
grips you, chills you
through to your very bones,
and how every sound
when you're underground
is some unspeakable thing
that groans.

It's the way
that you slip
on slime underfoot and it's
hard to remember the sun,
so when kids want to explore
all the caves on the shore
I say, 'Count me out.
It's no fun!'

Moira Andrew

Summer Fun

Sunshine,
All's fine.
In car,
Not far.
Park, ride,
Seaside.
On sand,
As planned.
Deckchair,
Take care.
Swim wear,
Somewhere.
Don't howl,
Found towel.
Beach clad,
Even dad.
Beach swim,
Water skim.
One splash,
All dash.
One shout,
All out.
Soaking wet,
No regret.
Water salty,
NOT my faulty.
Awful thirst,
Drink first.
Beach flop,
Lollipop.
Hot feet,
Lunch eat.
Mum burns,
Body turns.
Dad snores,
BOTH BORES!
Sand play,
HOORAY!
Real hassle,
Sand castle.
Bat, ball,
Sister call.
Run, catch,
No match.
¡Getting late,
Bus wait.
Goodbye,
Sea, sky.
SUMMER FUN,
NUMBER ONE!

Ian Souter

July is...

A flower unfolding
Heat haze fuzzing
Blossom scented
Bee buzzing
Glow of a month

John Cotton

TALKING TOGETHER

- **Holidays:** Holidays loom large in July - everyone anticipating the end of the school year. Talk about how best to use time away from school: making the most of good weather - cycling, skipping, skateboarding, walking. Encourage children away from indoor pursuits - plenty of time for computer games or television and video watching in the dark days of winter!

- Read Ian Souter's poem 'Summer Fun'. Talk about days by the sea: fun and games, disasters, picnics. Ask each group to list four funny things that have happened/might happen on an outing to the seaside. Illustrate each event, using and filling an A4 sheet. (See Writing Activities.)

- **Nature notebooks:** This is the final round-up for the year-long nature notebooks. Take time to tidy them up, check spelling, add any illustrations that have been missed, and arrange to have the books on display for Parents' Evening. Invite parents to read and admire the books with the authors on hand to talk about how and where they got their information.

- **Sports Day:** July is the month for Sports Day. Talk about what it means to train, week in, week out, as sports professionals have to do. If possible, arrange for a local athlete, footballer, cricketer, tennis player, sprinter, to talk with the children about aspects of training, winning, losing. Suggest to each group that they make up a set of questions to put to the athlete, so that he/she is able to make direct contact with the children.

- Make a display of sports days past and present. Read Gina Douthwaite's poem 'Spot-a, Spot-a Sports Day', where the last verse says *what a lot o' rain!/Not a spot o' sunshine./ Call it off, again.'* Find out how often this has happened over past years and make a graph of sports day weather, perhaps gleaning information from the school log book.

- **Seaside:** It might be possible to take the children on a day out to the sea - if so, July is perhaps the best month. No doubt such a trip will include paddling, pool-dipping and building sand castles.

- Encourage children to look and listen, to taste the salt in the air, feel sea water slip through their fingers, the difference in touch between dry and wet sand, feel the sea breeze on their faces.

- Before the trip, look through information books about life on the sea shore. Most sea creatures and marine plants can only survive in a narrow section of the shore. Talk about how different creatures survive and what they live on. Build up a chart showing where particular creatures live. Colour each zone or area lightly with coloured pencil and draw the seaweed and creatures who live there (worms, molluscs, crabs, etc.).

- Explore a rock pool. Look and draw, taking care not to disturb the creatures who make their homes there.

- **Make a sea food web.**

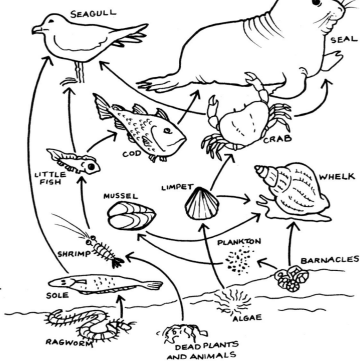

- Talk about the rubbish that often spoils our shoreline and discuss how it threatens wildlife. If your school is by the sea and the shore is polluted by litter, the class could take photographs and write letters to local newspapers about it. Councillors can also be contacted.

- Make sure that everyone is aware that the shore can be a dangerous environment and that all the children know to take care.

● In a very dry spell, when the crops needed rain, people sometimes used to make up prayers for rain. Talk about rain dances and prayers. Suggest making up prayers for St Swithin's Day - will it be a prayer for sunshine or a prayer for rain? Talk about famine and drought in countries like Somalia.

ASSEMBLIES
● **Congratulations:** Arrange an assembly to congratulate the children on their year-long nature notebook project. Perhaps a professional writer or illustrator could be invited to take part.
● Have an award ceremony (the mini-Booker prize!) for the Best Nature Notebook. (The local press might show an interest.) Small prizes can also be awarded for the most colourful notebook, the most informative, the neatest etc., so that children who are not necessarily best overall, can be winners.

● **Blessing the Waters:** This is a ceremony which has been taking place for over 100 years. It is held on the beach at Whitstable in Kent on 26th July and is attended by local fishermen and religious leaders. Everyone gathers to bless the sea and to thank God for fish and crabs and lobsters.
● Make and cut out silver fish, spotted crabs and pink lobsters. Hang a net in the hall and fill it with 'fruits of the sea'. Make up prayers of thanks and thread these through the net too.

● **Moving up and Moving on:** The end of the school year is a time of mixed emotions for both teachers and pupils, especially for those children who are leaving primary schools to move on to secondary education. The leaving assembly should be a time of thanksgiving for teachers and children who have shared a part of their lives over the past seven or so years.
● Suggest that leavers look at reception stage books and compare them with work at their own level to see how far they have come.
● Teachers can perhaps talk with the leavers about some of their *own* ambitions, fulfilled and unfulfilled, encouraging them to look ahead to the next stage of their schooling with confidence and with some excitement. Encourage the children to write about what they would like to achieve in the next few years, and as adults. Many will no doubt change their minds, but it is worth thinking about the future both in terms of the possible and the improbable!
● This is the time to quietly open up the envelopes sealed away in September. (See 'New Terms, New Faces', September). Ask the children if they would like to talk about their goals, whether they have achieved everything they set out to do, and if not, why not. Did they set unrealistic goals? Did something unexpected arise? Do they feel a certain amount of satisfaction and achievement?

● **Thank You:** Encourage the children to say 'Thank you' to the people who have helped them throughout the school year.
● The youngest children can make a frieze with painted figures cut out and glued in place with a 'Thank you' text added, e.g. *'Thank you, Mr Dodds, for helping us cross the road safely.' 'Thank you, Mrs Green, for making dinner for us every day.'*

GROUP ACTIVITIES
● **Seaweed:** On your trip to the seaside, ask each group to look for different kinds and colours of seaweed. Bring back a few strands of loose weed in a bottle of sea water and it will keep for several days. Use a seaside information book to identify your seaweeds and show on your zone chart where they belong.

● Seaweeds often have beautiful patterns, and some can be pressed like flowers. Float the seaweed in a tray of water and slip a piece of paper gently underneath. Use a paintbrush to arrange the fronds into an attractive pattern. Drain off excess water. Cover with an old handkerchief and place everything between sheets of newspaper under some heavy books. Leave to dry off for about a week. Mount, label and display.

● You can mount delicate feathery seaweed by floating on to paper as above. Then, when the paper is dry, cover the carefully arranged weed and paper with clear sticky-backed plastic. This is a tricky task and needs more than one pair of hands to do it successfully.

● **Swan Upping:** Find out as much as you can about swans. Look for information in books and wildlife sanctuary leaflets. Although very beautiful birds, they can deliver powerful blows with their wings when cornered or threatened. Make a book about swans, telling their life story.

● At one time all swans belonged to the sovereign. In the fifteenth century the Vintners and Dyers were granted the right to keep swans on the Thames. During the last few days of July, the ancient ceremony of Swan Upping takes place when that year's cygnets are rounded up and marked with notches on their bills: one notch for the Dyers, two notches (one each side of the bill) for the Vintners, with the Queen's cygnets left unmarked.

● If possible, visit the Swannery at Abbotsbury in Dorset. A swanherd has been in existence there since the sixteenth century.

● Listen to 'The Swan' by Saint-Säens (from 'The Carnival of the Animals'). Read Hans Christian Andersen's story of 'The Ugly Duckling'. Can you find any more music or stories about swans?

WRITING ACTIVITIES

● **Underwater:** Gather together pictures and information about the creatures of the deep, or find a poster of an underwater scene. Encourage children to think of images for each creature. Ask, not what they are, but what they look like: for example, dolphins like arrows or darts; whales like clubs or hammers; tiny coloured fish like flower petals or fireworks. Make a list of these ideas on the board, using *two* images only for each part of the picture. Move on to find appropriate movement words, for example, arrows *flying*, petals *floating*.

● Ask the children to write their own 'shopping list' on the 'borrow one idea from the board, find one of your own' basis. From the list, draft an underwater poem, beginning with their own images:

> *Like arrows, dolphins*
> *fly beneath the waves.*
> *Tiny coloured fish light*
> *the dark waters, like*
> *fireworks on Bonfire Night.*

● Edit the drafts and write the poems in best on blue or green paper, encouraging the children to work in the middle of the sheet, with an eye to design. From a top sheet, make a 'bubbly' frame and glue around the poem. (See photograph.)

Poems of the Underwater World

- **Caves:** Read Moira Andrew's poem 'Count me out'. Talk about how she feels about caves. Talk about the people who explore caves as a hobby. Talk about safety. Imagine exploring a deep dark cave. Think of what you would hear, how you would feel, what shadows you might see. Gather sets of words and ideas on the blackboard.
- Write an adventure story set in a cave. Imagine finding treasure, meeting pirates, getting lost. Use three main characters. Outline your story, so that you have an ending to work towards.
- Make a book, folded over, to reveal the inside of the cave. Write your story in and around the cave shape.
- Write an image poem about caves. Is a cave like a big black box? like an open mouth? like an empty treasure chest?

  > *A cave is like an open mouth*
  > *growling ferociously.*
  > *It is like an empty church*
  > *echoing eerily.*

  Display the poem inside a frame, as in the Underwater World idea, on page 69.

- **Summer Fun:** Read Ian Souter's poem 'Summer Fun'. Talk about marvellous holidays/holiday disasters. Write a letter to Grandma, your next-door neighbour, a penfriend, imagining that you are the child in Ian Souter's poem, telling them everything that happened on your day out. You can add a few ideas of your own to the letter.
- Use the ideas you thought of when you were talking together about *Summer Fun.* Each group can make a list poem of 'day out' disasters. Fit them beside the A4 illustrations and display 'the longest poem in the world' round the classroom wall.
- Write out a menu for your ideal picnic. Make a list of all the things you need to buy and work out how much it would cost for your family.

- **Renga of the Seaside:** A renga consists of several haiku on the same subject. This activity can be undertaken by a group, so that each child writes one haiku (five, seven, five syllables) arising from their seaside visit. One child might write about the harbour, another about a fishing boat, another about the seagulls overhead.
- Draw a picture of the harbour and fit the poems around it in appropriate places.

- **Write out a haiku or a mini-poem and display it in its own frame.**

- **July:** Read John Cotton's poem 'July is...'. He thinks of July as *'a flower unfolding'.* What other image could you use for July? an insect? a tree? a bird? Write a 'copycat' poem, using your new image for July, but keeping to the structure John Cotton has used.

- **The Ugly Duckling:** Read Hans Andersen's story. Look at some of the books which help the youngest children learn to read. Look at the language the authors have used. Retell *The Ugly Duckling* as a story for little children. Make a book and illustrate each page. Take your book to the reception class and read your story aloud.

Ship mobile, see Seaside Mobiles below   *Cave picture made of salt dough, see below*

● Read Gina Douthwaite's poem 'Spot-a, Spot-a Sports Day'. The poet has enjoyed juggling with words. Think of the races you run on sports day and make up a 'copycat' poem, keeping some of the rhythms from the original poem. Make it fun and enjoy playing with words - indeed, you might invent a few new words to use in your poem!

ART ACTIVITIES

● **Seaside mobiles:** Use basic instructions on page 10. Outline a sea scene inside a circle, and design a fishing boat, seagulls, a sand castle, in thin card and cut out to fit inside the circular frame. Hang from a loop of fine cotton and let the mobile swing in the breeze (see photograph above).

● **Count me out:** Using papier mâché, make a deep cave. Paint it in sombre colours. Add figures made of wire covered in paper strips and dipped in paste. Make your cave scene into a pirate hideout, an Aladdin's cave of hidden treasure, a cave full of *'unspeakable things that groan'.*

● Use salt dough (instructions on page 72) to make a cave picture (see photograph above).

● **Swan Upping:** Look at swans swimming, or look for pictures of swans. Each child can draw the outline of a swan - don't use a template. Cut it out, paint it white and leave to dry. Make 'feathers' from torn tissue paper. Beginning at the swan's tail, carefully glue the end of each feather down so that they overlap. For the best effect, don't screw up the tissue paper, but paste it flat.

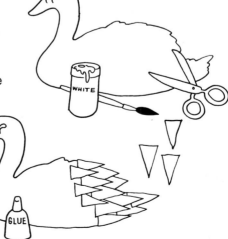

● Make a river background and glue on the fleet of swans, all swimming in one direction. Add bullrushes and a bridge. You might also want to show the Dyers and Vintners - even the Queen watching the Royal swans!

RECIPE FOR SALT DOUGH

3 cups plain flour
I cup cooking salt
I cup water
I teaspoon cooking oil

- Make a dough by mixing all the ingredients together in a bowl. Turn out on to a floured board and knead. Don't work the dough immediately, but put into a polythene bag and leave for about an hour.
- To use, break off a lump of dough approximately the size you think you will need. Leave the rest inside the polythene bag until it is required.
- Work directly on to a baking tray, concentrating on the basic shape. Add details (arms, legs, wings, etc.) by shaping on the board and using a little water to fix these to the main shape, as you would with pastry dough.
- You can create texture by marking with a fork or by pressing buttons, leaves, shells, bark, lace, etc. into the dough.
- Bake for about an hour at I50°C, 300°F, Gas Mark 2. Look at the back of the figure to make sure it is completely baked.
- Dry out for a day before colouring. Use poster paints for the best effect, then varnish on both sides using clear polyurethane. This step is necessary to preserve the baked dough. To apply the varnish, lay the model on the inside of a polythene shopping bag, opened out, and work first on the back. Two coats of varnish might be necessary.

REFERENCES
Festivals and Celebrations, by Rowland Purton, Blackwell Education, first published I982.
Fensterbilder, by Renate Vogl, Augustus Verlag, Germany.
Salt Dough Models, by Sue Organ, first published by Search Press Ltd., I993.

The author and publishers wish to thank the following who have kindly given permission for the use of copyright material: John Coldwell for The'First Day with a New Teacher', 'Snow Problem' and 'Racing my Shadow', John Cotton for 'July', Gina Douthwaite for 'Winter Window', 'Spot-a, Spot-a Sports Day' and 'Mad March Sun', John Foster for 'November', 'Chinese New Year Dragon' and 'It's spring' Michael Henry for 'Jack o'Lantern' Gerda Mayer for 'May Poem', first published in *Expression,* 1967 Tony Mitton for 'Diwali', first published in *Festivals,* compiled by Jill Bennett, 1994, Scholastic Collections, David R. Morgan for 'June Tune', Brian Moses for 'New Beginning', 'Windy Playground' from *Knock Down Ginger,* 1994, Cambridge University Press, and 'Hatching Eggs' from *Hippopotamus Dancing,* 1994, Cambridge University Press, Judith Nicholls for 'Where was the Colour Orange Born?' and 'May Day' Joan Poulson for 'leaf-birds', 'Magpie World' and 'Like Purple Aeroplanes' Irene Rawnsley for 'Strange Fruit', 'Don't forget the birds', 'The Sun's Game' and 'Rain' Rita Ray for '24 Windows on the Advent Calendar', Sheila Simmons for 'Grass Music', Ian Souter for 'Bonfire Night Lights', 'Christmas is...' and 'Summer Fun', Charles Thomson for 'Blackberries', John Walsh for 'Sky Arrows' and 'Snow-stroll'

The publishers would also like to thank Moira Andrew for the inclusion of copyright material, as follows: 'October', 'December's Dawn', 'January', 'Flamenco', 'Rainbows'; and 'Spring in the City', 'Autumn Treasure' and 'Images of May', first published by Nelson; and for 'Autumn Sorrow', 'The Christmas Star', 'Portrait of a Dragon', 'Nature Study' and 'Count me out', first published by OUP.

For details of further Belair Publications
please write to:
BELAIR PUBLICATIONS LTD
P.O. Box 12 TWICKENHAM TW1 2QL England

For sales and distribution (outside USA and Canada):
FOLENS PUBLISHERS,
Albert House, Apex Business Centre,
Boscombe Road, Dunstable, Bedfordshire, LU5 4RL
England.

For sales and distribution in USA and Canada:
Belair Publications USA, 116 Corporation Way, Venice, Florida, 34292, USA.